At Pentecost

At Pentecost
Charles Ludwig

Warner Press, Inc.

Anderson, Indiana

Published by
Warner Press, Inc.
Anderson, Indiana

All scripture passages, unless otherwise indicated, are from the King James Version or The Holy Bible, New International Version. Copyright © 1973, 1978, 1984 International Bible Society. Used by permission of Zondervan Bible Publishers.

Copyright © 1991 by Warner Press, Inc.
ISBN #0-87162-603-9
Stock #D8151
All Rights Reserved
Printed in the United States of America
Warner Press, Inc.

Arlo F. Newell, Editor in Chief
Dan Harman, Book Editor
Cover by David Liverett

Note: All italics in scripture quotations in this book have been added by the author for emphasis.

Other books from Warner Press by Charles Ludwig:
- Wonderful Jesus (1942)
  The Adventures of Juma (1944)
  Witch Doctor's Holiday (1945)
  Christ at the Door (1946)
  Leopard Glue (1946)
  Sankey Still Sings (1947)
  Cannibal Country (1948)
  Mama Was a Missionary (1963)
  On Target (1963)
  Spinning Shoes (1988)
  At the Cross (1989)
  At the Tomb (1991)

Dedication

For my sister-in-law, Ruth Hnida, who has been a blessing for more than half a century.

Table of Contents

Preface x

Chapter

1. Jesus' "Wait" Meant "Go!" 1
2. The Pause that Transformed Uganda 11
3. Who Is the Holy Spirit? 21
4. The Holy Spirit in the Old Testament 33
5. Old Testament Pentecost 43
6. The Rooster That Changed the World 51
7. Peter's Bitter, Bitter Cup................... 61
8. Even So They Went Fishing................. 71
9. They Waited, and Waited, and Waited 81
10. Pentecost! 91
11. The Holy Spirit's Ministry 103
12. The Holy Spirit Baptism Is for *All* Believers .. 117

Epilogue 129

Answers to *Can You Answer?* 133

Notes.. 140

Bibliography................................... 141

Preface

The most stimulating statements ever made on our behalf were made by the sandal-clad man from Galilee—Jesus Christ, *the* Son of God!

One of these statements that did—and *still* could!—transform the world, was made by him as he faced the sorrowing eleven in the Upper Room. This is how eyewitness John recorded it:

> But I tell you the truth: It is for your good that I am going away. Unless I go away, the Counselor will not come to you; but if I go, I will send him to you (16:7, NIV).

Those words must have staggered the eleven, for they had left all to follow Jesus. During their years of training they had laughed with him, eaten with him, traveled with him, been instructed by him and rebuked by him; and, on one memorable occasion, he had even paid impulsive Peter's taxes.

But what did that incredible statement mean?

It meant that Jesus, imprisoned in his physical body, could only be at a single place at a single time. In contrast, the Holy Spirit, also known as the Counselor, the Comforter, and by many other titles, could be at all places and in all hearts at the same time.

Although John Wesley wrote, "I look upon the whole world as my parish," he was forced to immediately add, "I mean, that in whatever part of it I am, I judge it my . . . duty, to declare unto all that are willing to hear, the glad tidings of salvation" (Wesley, 201).

The Holy Spirit is *not* confined to one place but rather has many tasks. Any of those tasks can be performed simultaneously if the Spirit so chooses. Moreover, the Spirit can abide and work in any of our hearts at any time and in any place if we allow him to do so.

He convicted Jim Irwin while Jim was on the moon!

Overwhelmed by the omniscience and omnipresence of the Holy Spirit, Paul exclaimed, "Don't you know that you yourselves are God's temple and that God's Spirit lives in you?" (1 Cor. 3:16, NIV).

The fact that the Holy Spirit, the Third Person of the Trinity can lead and comfort us, and be within us should make us feel even more overwhelmed than Luther felt when he offered his first mass.

Referring to that occasion, Luther remembered: "Soon in most solemn tones, I recited the words: 'We offer unto thee, the living, the true, the eternal God.' At these words I was utterly stupefied and terror-stricken. I thought to myself, 'With what tongue shall I address such Majesty, seeing that all men ought to tremble in the presence of even an earthly prince? Who am I, that I should lift up mine eyes or raise my hands to such divine Majesty? The angels surround Him. At His nod the earth trembles. And shall I, a miserable little pygmy, say, 'I want this, I ask for that?' For I am dust and ashes and full of sin, and I am speaking to the living and eternal God" (Ludwig, 1986, 56).

Prophesying the coming advent of the Holy Spirit, on the "last and greatest day of the Feast [the Passover], Jesus stood and said in a loud voice, "If any man is thirsty, let him come to me and drink. Whoever believes in me, as the Scripture has said, streams of living water will flow from within him' " (John 7:37-38, NIV).

In the next verse John explained: "By this he meant the Spirit, whom those who believed in him were later to receive."

On another occasion, John quoted Jesus as saying, "[The Holy Spirit] dwelleth with you, *and shall be in you*" (14:17).

That is a stupendous saying! Regrettably many Christians are unaware of this truth. Others are frightened by obscurantists who, buttressed by passages such as "that thou hast hid these things from the wise and prudent, and hast revealed them unto babes" (Luke 10:21) are convinced that their ideas are always correct. Unfortunately, many such persons believe that a personal experience or impression is more trustworthy than the plain teachings of the Bible.

The fact that millions of Christians miss the blessings that God has laid up for them because of a fallen TV evangelist, an obscurantist, or one who confuses an impression with plain biblical truth, is a tragedy of our time just as it was in the early church. At that time, John was extremely definite: "Dear friends, do not believe every spirit, but test the spirits to see whether they are from God, because many false prophets have gone out into the world" (1 John 4:1, NIV).

One fact is evident. All large congregations are not Spirit-filled; and all Spirit-filled congregations are not large. Nonetheless all Spirit-filled Christians and Spirit-filled assemblies prove that they are Spirit-filled by bearing fruit. What are the fruits? Numbers? Not quite! Paul identified them as "love, joy, peace, patience, kindness, goodness, faithfulness, gentleness and self control" (Gal. 5:22-23, NIV).

Since we want to be biblical, we shall study the occasion of the New Testament Pentecost objectively and try, without bias, to see what happened on that occasion. As in *At the Cross* and *At the Tomb* we will follow each chapter with a series of questions and provide answers in the appendix. This format is designed to make *At Pentecost* an ideal book for personal and group study.

1

Jesus' "Wait" Meant Go!

At the end of their three-year course, the eleven disciples were all but staggered at the central word in Jesus' final command. This is so because of the occasion and because they had only heard him use that pivotal word on one previous occasion.

(On that singular first occasion, he had merely used it as a verb in a parable, *not* as a command. See Luke 12:36).

That explosive word was *wait!* (Acts 1:4).

The eleven—Judas was already dead—were astounded because their course of training had ended with the most glorious climax with which any period of training could possibly end. Graduates that they were, it must have seemed to them that instead of saying *wait*, Jesus would have all but shouted Go! Go! Go!

Consider what the eleven apostles had experienced during those last forty days. Following his crucifixion Jesus had periodically appeared to them in person.*

He had passed through a solid wall. He had eaten with them. He had baked fish for them. They had seen him walk on the water. He "breathed on them and said, 'Receive the Holy Spirit' " (John 20:22, NIV).

(F. F. Bruce enlivened this incident by pointing out that "the verb used here (*emphysaō*) is that used in the

[Septuagint] of Gen. 2:7 where, after fashioning the first man from dust, God 'breathed into his face the breath of life, and the man became a living soul,' " [392]).

In addition, Jesus had demonstrated the power of going by sending out the seventy as recorded in Luke 10:1-18; and those seventy were so overjoyed by their success that they exclaimed: "Even the devils are subject unto us through thy name" (v. 17).

Surely, with all these experiences, the disciples should have been ready to go just as Matthew had indicated. Nonetheless, Jesus didn't think so; and so *after* his previous "GO!" (Matthew 28:19), he now said *"wait!"* Why?

Puzzled, one can almost hear Peter saying, "He told us to go when we were on the mountain! C-could i-it be that he wants us to wait because even after his appearances we went f-f-f-fishing?"

That wasn't the answer! Jesus had not lost faith in them. We know this, for he appeared to them again on that very occasion while they were still frustrated in the midst of their unsuccessful fishing expedition (John 21:3).

Perhaps the best answer for Jesus' command for them to *wait* has been pointed out by G. Campbell Morgan. According to him, the most potent word in Acts 1:1 is *began*.

If this is so, and I believe it is, it indicates that the Acts of the Apostles do not record all that Jesus had said nor all the miracles he would perform in the future.

That first verse reads: "The former treatise have I made, O Theophilus, of all that Jesus *began* both to do and teach" (Acts 1:1). If it were not for that word *began*, to which Morgan has drawn our attention, we might conclude that Luke had recorded *all* that Jesus had both said and done. But that is *not* the case. This is so, for Jesus hasn't stopped speaking to his children. In our time, as all of us know, he has continued to work miracles (Morgan 8-11).

Luke's *Acts of the Apostles* is merely the first installment of a serial that will continue until the Lord brings it to an end.

It was, and is, the will of Christ that the work that he *began* should continue throughout the ages. This is what he meant in his breathtaking statement as recorded in John 14:12:

> Verily, verily, I say unto you, he that believeth on me, the works that I do shall he do also; and *greater* works than these shall he do; because I go unto my Father (John 14:12).

Notice that this passage, given in the Upper Room and recorded by John who stood nearby, is addressed to "he that believeth on me." Thus, if you are a believer, that means it is addressed to *you*!

In preparing the Twelve for the time when he would be crucified, resurrected, and finally ascend to the Father, Jesus had spent nearly three years strengthening them for those events.

Like teachers of the time, he did not appropriate a classroom for his followers. Instead, he led them from place to place. He taught lessons in the open. Some in or from a boat, others at the top or side of a mountain or in a wilderness. Additional lessons were taught on roof tops, beneath the trees, and both outside and inside the temple.

This outside "classroom" was not always the pleasant and well-tended country that tourists visit. In the dry season from May to October, as Jesus and the Twelve walked from village to village, or from city to city, they encountered dust, empty, or at least stale cisterns, parched fields, and desolation.

And, as in the land of the Masai, flies and insects abounded. They swarmed into peoples' eyes, crept into their eyes and mouths, and in that screens had not been invented, they settled on and contaminated the food. They were such a nuisance that often, as the people shooed them away, they accused them of being under the control of Beelzebub, identified by some as a Philistine god designated in Ekron as "Lord of the Flies."

When nature called, people relieved themselves in any semiprivate place—behind a tree or a stone or in the grass. Lacking sanitary facilities, the people lived in a land dominated by plagues, intestinal worms, and other diseases such as leprosy and smallpox.

Superstition was king. Moreover, those who reached forty years of age were considered old.

In *The Life and Times of Jesus the Messiah*, Alfred Edersheim related the magic cure for boils. Victims were advised by their physicians to repeat the following incantation:

> Paz, Baziya, Mas, Masiva, Kas, Kasiya Sharlai and Amarial—Ye Angels that come from the land of Sodom to heal painful boils! Let the color not become more red, let it not farther spread, let its seed be absorbed in the belly. As a mule does not propagate itself, so let not this evil propagate itself in the body of M. the son of M (775).

Other diseases, including blindness, were to be cured by means of this procedure:

> After having made a chord from the hair of some animal one end [should] be tied to the foot of the patient, and the other to that of a dog. Children [should then] strike [the] pieces of crockery behind the dog, while the patient repeats these words: "The dog is old and the cock is foolish."
>
> Next seven pieces of meat [were] to be taken from seven different houses and hung up on the doorposts.
>
> The dog [it was then prescribed, was to] eat the meat on a dunghill in an open place. Lastly the chord [was] to be untied. [Then, they were told they] should repeat [the following magic words]: "Let the blindness of M. the son of N. leave M. the son of N. and pierce the eyeballs of the dog!" (775).

Along with poverty, beggars, and lepers crying "Unclean!

Unclean!" there was the constant aggravation of being ruled by Rome. Sometimes this aggravation was personalized by a Roman soldier who, after threatening with his spear, might say: "Hey, you! Take my load. Carry it for a mile."

Backgrounded by all of this, Jesus taught the Twelve along with those who came to listen, and, being the greatest of all teachers, he spoke in parables, used simple words, and often made use of background with which his listeners could identify. He did this in order to make his message more easily understood.

George Whitefield also used background to further the power of his sermons. As he stood to preach in Boston,

> darkening columns crowded the bright sunny sky . . . and swept their shadows over the building. . . .
> "See that emblem of human life," he said, as he pointed to a flitting shadow. "It paused for a moment, and concealed the brightness of heaven from our view; but it is gone. And, where will you be, my hearers, when your lives have passed away like that dark cloud?" (Beldon, n.p.).

We have numerous examples of the way Jesus used background:

"A certain man had two sons . . ." "Behold, there went out a sower to sow." "Whosoever shall compel thee to go a mile, go with him twain." (One mile was the legal limit).

When he found himself sitting on the edge of Jacob's well, he made use of a law that he had stated and that Paul later quoted: "It is more blessed to give than to receive" (Acts 20:35). In requesting a drink he filled the woman with goodwill, as she complied with his request (John 4:7). He used this exchange to ask questions and preach a sermon: "But whosoever drinketh of the water that I shall give him shall never thirst; but the water that I shall give him shall be in him a well of water springing up into everlasting life" (John 4:14).

During the Feast of Tabernacles, celebrated toward the beginning of October, Jesus had an extraordinarily ideal occasion at which he could preach a doctrine or make statements that would help mold Israel until his Second Coming. This was so because

1. The Feast of Tabernacles, also known as the Feast of Ingathering (Exodus 23:16; 34:22), was one of the great annual festivals that God had decreed.
2. All males—including slaves!—were required to participate. This meant that a huge throng was always present. Thus it was an ideal time for Jesus to bare his heart.
3. Since the harvest had already been gathered, and the Day of Atonement had been concluded five days before, those who attended knew that their sins had been canceled. Spiritually cleansed, they were in an exuberant mood.

Moreover, their ecstatic spirits were brightened by a full moon. In addition, they were living in booths as Moses had commanded—booths that had been erected to commemorate the way the Lord had taken care of them in the wilderness (Lev. 23:42). All this invigorated them with confidence that the Lord would continue to take care of them.

4. This feast was a time of unbelievable joy. During the week, sacrifice followed sacrifice. As the coals on the altar glowed and the smoke of the sacrifice twisted upward on each day, the priests marched in procession around the altar. As they marched, they expressed their joy by singing Psalm 118:25 "O Lord, save us; O Lord, grant us success" (NIV).

Alfred Edersheim describes the ceremony:

> But on the seventh, "that great day of the feast," they made the circuit of the altar seven times, remembering how the walls of Jericho had fallen in similar circumstances, and anticipating how, by the direct interposition of God, the walls of heathenism would fall before Jehovah.
> It was on that day, after the priest had returned

from Siloam with his golden pitcher and for the last time poured its contents to the base of the altar, [that the people responded in a tempestuous finale] (1950, 281).

During this procedure, the enthusiasm of the people kept rising higher and higher as one activity led to another. At one point, a section of the throng from near the altar began to wave leafless branches while the entire congregation chanted verses from the Egyptian Hallel—Psalm 113-118. (These praise-psalms were so named because they traced God's activity among them from the time of their exodus from Egypt).

One can almost hear them now as they, accompanied by flutes, began to sing those sixty-seven verses of praise that began:

> Praise ye the Lord, Praise O ye servants of the Lord. Blessed be the name of the Lord from this time forth and forevermore. From the rising of the sun until the going down of the sun the Lord's name is to be praised.

With memories of Egypt, the Red Sea, the Wilderness and Jericho's tumbling walls in their minds they must have been stirred in a far greater depth than anyone has ever been stirred even by Verdi's "Triumphal March" in *Aida*.

Then after the final verse (Psalm 118:29), Jesus stood up and those who knew and loved him were stirred even more. As he stood there in his spotless gown and personal purity, the Twelve must have wondered what he would say, for with the vast multitude surrounding him he was faced with a rare opportunity to enunciate something vital.

As he remained quiet for a long moment, the Twelve must have wondered what doctrine he would declare. While we relive this occasion in our time, we wonder why he didn't teach them something about how to stop the diseases that riddled their land. Such a lesson would have been most appropriate!

In that the mortality rate was high because of typhoid, he might have said, "If you will boil the water before you drink it, you will escape the disease that is killing so many."

Or he might have said, "Many of your children are dead on their feet. They have large stomachs, pasty-looking faces, lackluster eyes. They are full of worms. Worm eggs spread because you lack sanitary conditions.

"When nature calls, you relieve yourself wherever you can, and so those vile eggs in your system are passed on to others. You must change this. You must dig latrines."

Jesus, of course, knew all of this, just as he knows the cure for cancer. Moreover, he knew that his words would be accepted by even his worst enemies, because everyone knew that he had power to heal.

But instead of talking about hygiene, as he viewed the dense masses before him and the booths on the rooftops and in the street, he talked about "living water." In doing this, was he like a surgeon who, with a dying man bleeding to death on the operating table, neglects the dying man in order to speak to his students about the culture of roses? Not at all.

According to John 7:38 in the NIV, Jesus said:

> If anyone is thirsty, let him come to me and drink.
> Whoever believes in me, as the Scripture has said,
> streams of living water will flow from within him.

This was the same message he had given to the woman in Samaria, a message that had instigated revival; and many of his hearers understood it, for they also had tasted his living water.

In our time, Malcolm Muggeridge, converted to Christ near the age of seventy after having spent his life scoffing at Christianity, has let us know the effect that this living water had on him:

> I may, I suppose, regard myself or pass for being a relatively successful man. People occasionally stare at me in the streets—that's fame. I can fairly

easily earn enough to qualify for admission to the higher slopes of the Internal Revenue—that's success. Furnished with money and a little fame, even the elderly, if they care to, may partake of trendy diversions—that's pleasure. It might happen once in a while that something I said or wrote was sufficiently heeded for me to persuade myself that it represented a serious impact on our time—that's fulfillment.

Yet I say to you—and beg you to believe me—multiply these tiny triumphs by a million, add them all together, and they are nothing—less than nothing, a positive impediment—measured against one draught of that living water Christ offers to the spiritually thirsty, irrespective of who they are" (Porter, n.p.).

Yes, living water is pure, potent—and everlasting. But in our time, *after* Pentecost, it is even more potent than it was to the Woman at the Well, this is because now it can not only quench our thirst; but, in *addition*, "streams of living water will flow from within him," promised Jesus (John 7:38, NIV).

John explained this in the next verse: "By this he meant the Spirit, whom those who believed in him were later to receive. Up to that time the Spirit had not been given, since Jesus had not yet been glorified."

Was Jesus mistaken in talking about living water rather than hygiene at the Feast of Tabernacles? Again we must thunder with a definite no. Why? For numerous reasons, one of which is that many who have made the greatest advances in medical discoveries, advances that have doubled our longevity since the time of the Roman Empire, were men and women who had tasted the living water *and out of whose inward parts had flowed* "streams of living water."

But there are yet two other reasons why Jesus said wait to the Eleven.

1. They were to wait in order that prophecy might be

fulfilled. John the Baptist had prophesied: "I baptize you with water for repentance. But after me will come one who is more powerful than I, whose sandals I am not fit to carry. *He will baptize you with the Holy Spirit and with fire.*" (Matthew 3:11, NIV). This had not yet taken place, for even though Jesus had "breathed on them, and said, 'Receive the Holy Spirit' " (John 20:22, NIV) a cleansing fire was not even mentioned.

2. Jesus himself delayed beginning his ministry until he had been both baptized in water and filled with the Holy Spirit. Matthew recorded the occasion: "As soon as Jesus was baptized, he went up out of the water. At that moment heaven was opened, and he saw the Spirit of God descending like a dove and lighting on him. And a voice from heaven said, "This is my Son, whom I love; with him I am well pleased" (3:16-17, NIV).

The manifestation of the entire Trinity on that occasion is significant.

Can You Answer?
1. John used the Greek word *emphysaō* for "breathed" when he described how Jesus breathed on the disciples. That word was also used in Genesis 2:7. On what occasion was that?
2. What ministries did Jesus commission the Seventy to perform? Did they succeed?
3. Which members of the Trinity were present when Jesus was baptized?
4. On that occasion, what was the form in which the Holy Spirit presented himself when he descended on Jesus? Who witnessed the descent of the Holy Spirit?
5. How old was Jesus when he began his ministry? How do we know?
6. Does the Acts of the Apostles include all the works that Jesus accomplished through his followers? If not, what word in Acts 1:1 would indicate otherwise?
7. What were the sanitary conditions in Israel at this time? Did the Jews try to heal themselves by repeating incantations? Why did Jesus emphasize matters of the Spirit instead of simple hygiene?

2

The Pause That Transformed Uganda

Since obedience to the Holy Spirit can transform believers, entire congregations—and even entire nations—Satan detests and fears the power of the Holy Spirit even more than we fear poison gas or the hydrogen bomb. Moreover, being an experienced fighter, Satan knows the most useful way to minimize the effectiveness of the Holy Spirit among the followers of Christ.

One of his ways to minimize the power of the Holy Spirit is to encourage Christians to quarrel over technical aspects of doctrine. This fact is painfully evident. The Roman emperor Julian the Apostate (331-363), so called because he tried to restore pagan worship, was unquestionably one of Satan's most effective tools.

Clever man that he was, Julian decided that the best way to destroy Christians was to allow Christians to destroy one another through debates over fine points of doctrine.

And so, pretending to have achieved a new tolerance, he summoned back the bishops he had banished and restored them to their parishes.

As these men streamed back to their former fields of labor, he ridiculed them by declaring that he was sorry for the "poor, blind, deluded Galileans, who forsook the most glorious privilege of man, the worship of the immortal gods, and instead of the [immortal gods] worshiped dead men's bones."

Julian often ordered antagonistic bishops to debate an issue in his presence. Then, as the dispute grew in intensity, he egged them on for his own amusement. He often said: "No wild beasts are so fierce and irreconcilable as the Galilean sectarians."

Today, many Christians who could make their lives count are shackled in the same trap, and, unfortunately, many of the quarrels that destroy them are over such questions as these:

- When does a believer receive the Holy Spirit?
- Is there a difference between having the Holy Spirit "with you" and "in you?" (John 14:17).
- What *is* the baptism of the Holy Spirit?
- Does one have to tarry to receive the baptism?
- How can one know that he or she has received the infilling of the Holy Spirit? Is speaking in unknown tongues the only evidence? Are other evidences sufficient?
- What is the meaning of eradication? What does eradication accomplish? Does it root out the old stump?

Such questions are *extremely* important. Jesus was explicit: "All manner of sin and blasphemy shall be forgiven unto men: *but the blasphemy against the Holy Ghost shall not be forgiven unto men*" (Matthew 12:31).

Luke indicated the priority Jesus held in regard to being filled with the Spirit (Acts 1:7-8). On that occasion, after he had been asked: "Lord, wilt thou at this time restore again the kingdom to Israel?" (v. 6), he replied immediately: "It is not for you to know the times or the seasons, which the Father hath put in his own power. *But ye shall receive power, after the Holy Ghost is come upon you: and ye shall be witnesses.*"

Our purpose in this chapter, however, is not to discuss each of these and other questions. Like the atonement of Christ, no one can completely understand it, and yet we accept it and experience it, and exclaim about the "living water" we have tasted.

It is thus with the Holy Spirit. We cannot completely understand the mathematics of the Trinity; and yet we can experience the infilling of the Holy Spirit and notice what has happened to others in our age and other ages who have been baptized with the Holy Spirit.

(In other chapters we will discuss who the Holy Spirit is; where he originated; the Holy Spirit's personality; work; and, especially, how we can experience the Holy Spirit baptism. But here we want to understand what the Holy Spirit has done and *can* do in our time.)

Because of this objective, let's turn the calendar back to the 1890s and notice what happened to Anglican, George Pilkington, when he was baptized with the Holy Spirit.

A handsome, six-foot double blue from Cambridge, whose brilliant mind had enabled him to attend that famous school on a scholarship, had been deeply moved by the meetings of Moody and Sankey at Cambridge. Convinced that he should be a missionary, he eventually decided to go to Uganda.

At the time, Uganda was on the lips of many in missionary circles. After having "found" Livingstone, H. M. Stanley returned to Africa. In 1875 he pushed north to Uganda. There, he was amazed to find an organized nation. The Baganda not only had a king, the *kabaka*, but also a royal family and a prime minister, the *katikiro*. In addition, unlike the almost naked tribes they had passed in Kenya, the Baganda were fully clothed.*

Their garments were made of *embugu*, (bark-cloth).

This reddish-brown fabric was manufactured by hammering figtree bark until it widened into cloth. Toga-fashion the men knotted their robes on the right shoulder while the women wrapped yards of the material around their chests just under their arms.

The upper classes even wore locally manufactured shoes!

Thoroughly impressed, Stanley made an appointment with King Mutesa. His Majesty was an eager listener and asked to be taught the doctrines of Christianity. After Stanley had exhausted the little knowledge he had, Mutesa had a letter addressed to Queen Victoria in which he begged that missionaries be sent to Uganda.

Since this was before post offices, Stanley sent the letter north by means of a Belgian, Linants de Bellefonds. Unfortunately, Bellefonds and his group were attacked by the Bari tribe, and he was murdered. Later, when an expeditionary force went south to investigate the massacre, they found Bellefonds' remains; and in one of his high-knee Wellington boots, they discovered Mutesa's letter.

The letter was immediately forwarded to General Gordon, the one who located the Garden Tomb in Jerusalem. General Gordon relayed it to England.

Published in the *Daily Telegraph*, the letter caused a sensation. Almost immediately, a gentleman who dubbed himself an "Unprofitable Servant," mailed five thousand pounds to the Committee for the use of the Church Missionary Society. Other checks followed.

Straightaway eight highly qualified men were accepted to become missionaries in Uganda.

Heat, disease, and hostile natives riddled their ranks as they trudged on their six-hundred mile journey from Zanzibar to Mengo, the capital, now known as Kampala. Since Mackay, a young engineer, and one of the original eight had to remain on the coast because of illness, and Smith and O'Neil had been slain, only Wilson was able to remain, and he left before he had been in Uganda for an entire year.

During the year Wilson remained in Uganda, he realized that the nation was not as far advanced as Stanley had been led to believe. Superstition had a solid grip on the people, and Mutesa ruled with a firm and bloody hand. Heeding the advice of a witch doctor, Mutesa ordered the members of an entire village drowned in the lake in order to cure the queen's toothache.

Mukajangwa, the head executioner, always remained close to Mutesa in order to immediately obey any order His Majesty might announce. When the pages in his court refused to eat the meat he had provided, declaring that since the cow had not been killed by a Muslim, its flesh was only fit for dogs, Mutesa lost his temper.

"So my meat is only fit for dogs?" he challenged, as he summoned his executioner. "Go, at once," he bellowed, "and arrest every uncircumcised man or boy and bring them here!" Mukajangwa and his subordinates went to work immediately.

Each of the death squad wore a cap with black strings hanging over their faces which were to make them appear even more terrifying. By evening two hundred were brought in. All were burned alive.

Mutesa did not always have his victims killed. His orders were sometimes more gentle: "Cut off his nose!" "Slash off his ears!" "Hack off his fingers!" "Chop off his right hand!"

Mutesa died in 1884 and was honored by being the first king of Uganda to be buried in a coffin. The missionaries, both French Catholic and British Protestant, were delighted that Mutesa was followed to the throne by his eighteen-year-old son Mwanga, rather than by his eldest son Kalema, who was dreaded for his cruelty.

Mwanga had sat at the feet of both the Protestant and Catholic missionaries. On several occasions, he had even discussed the possibility of being baptized. He was revered by his subjects as *Mutefu* ("The Mild").

Alas, Mwanga's "mildness" like that of Nero, didn't last. Influenced by Muslims who didn't like the way the British interfered with their slave trade, and alarmed by the Germans who had annexed Tanganyika, Mwanga decided to exterminate Christianity in Uganda.

Cruel tyrant that he was, his usual method was to order his victims burned to death. Hundreds—some after their arms had been slashed off with a panga—perished in the flames.

These perils did not stop the influx of missionaries to Uganda. Believing in "safety last," Bishop Hannington ignored the many warnings he had heard, and headed toward Uganda and his ultimate martyrdom. Afraid that Hannington was coming to Uganda in order to seize the country, Mwanga ordered that he and his entire caravan of porters be put to death.

Hannington was killed on October 29, 1885. His last words received in England and scribbled by him by the light of a campfire were: "If this is the last chapter of my earthly history, then the next will be the first page of the heavenly—no blots and smudges, no incoherence, but sweet converse in the presence of the Lamb!"

George Pilkington knew about the martyrdoms, but they did not deter him. God had given him the gift of mastering languages quickly, and he was determined to use this gift for the advancement of the work of Christ in Uganda.

Friends in England remembered his last days among them—days filled with public speeches for the benefit of Uganda. One man who had heard him speaking to a group of boys in a drawing room reminisced:

> I can see him now—his tall, upright figure, his solemn face, standing out against the background of wallpaper in the meeting room at Worcester Lodge. . . . He told the boys how useless it was, and how wearying, to tie fruit on a fruitless tree—the nature of the tree must be changed. He described himself as not being the same person since his conversion—in fact as almost literally someone else, a new creation (Battersby 45).

On January 23, 1890, Pilkington, along with other "Cambridge men" sailed for Africa on the *Karparthala*.

As bloody as he was, Mwanga had a certain fear of Queen Victoria whom he called "Queeni." Also, he liked Mackay. This young engineer's accomplishments completely baffled the Baganda. When he rolled logs up a hill, they watched in amazement, for they, like the American Indians, were unacquainted with the rolling action of a wheel. As they stared, they shouted: "*Mackay lubare. Mackay lubare!* Mackay is the great spirit!"

The *katikiro* informed Mackay that he was a favorite at court and even asked him to marry his daughter!

Because of Mwanga's fascination with Mackay, the missionaries enjoyed a period of safety. During this period Pilkington, having learned the language from a porter on the way from the coast, translated the Bible into Luganda and Mackay printed it on his miniature press.

The Baganda were utterly fascinated by the paper that could talk. Because of this, the Luganda Bible enjoyed a brisk sale, even though it sold for five hundred cowrie shells—the currency of Uganda, which required three months of hard work to earn.

This Bible was so revered, the Baganda sat around campfires as a leader read it to them and thus taught the listeners to read. Those on the opposite side of the fire learned to read upside down!

Arthur Fisher, one of seven missionaries, had sailed for Uganda in 1892. Because Fisher was one of the last veterans of the mission staff alive in the early 1950s, David P. Mannix went to his home in Eastbourne on the southeast coast of England to interview him. "His first station was near Mityana," wrote Mannix, "a community some fifty miles west of Mengo. The local chief hated missionaries. But . . . the simple eloquence of the young Irishman soon won him over. Weeping, the chief begged to be baptized. 'I want to be called Saul because I, too, persecuted the Christians.' " Glad at so easy a victory, Fisher promised to accept him into the fold and retired to sleep in a straw hut the chief had built for him. Mannix continues, "That night the chief got roaring drunk . . . and shot the hut full of burning arrows.

" 'I had a good deal of trouble with that old man,' Mr. Fisher admitted regretfully. 'He would get converted every day and at night get drunk and set fire to whatever hut I was sleeping in. After the third time I lost patience. I took off my coat, rolled up my sleeves and went and had a heart-to-heart talk with him. After that, we got along very well' " (Hunter and Mannix 68-69).

Later, Fisher founded what eventually became Makerere College.

In spite of sporadic opposition, the work of Christ grew.

Many chiefs became Christians and numerous congregations built meetinghouses that were crowded to the doors. Thousands learned to read. Moreover, the message of Christ as proclaimed by the earliest pioneers had already had an effect on the Royal Family. This was indicated by the events that followed the death of King Mutesa. Instead of the old ritual, Mutesa had a Western-type burial.

In the past, according to Ashe: "The corpse of the deceased king in former times was taken to a place called *Merera* . . . some eight hours' march west of Mengo. Here the lower jaw was cut off and placed in an ant-heap, that the ants may eat it perfectly clean. The body, despoiled of the lower jaw, was not interred, but carried to the house of a peasant on the estate, and laid there; the house was immediately broken down, so that the heavy thatch . . . might completely cover the dead king's corpse. . . . Then the chief's butler or brewer or cook, the chief of the . . . herds-men, and the second in command were put to death there. The third ruler was left alive; but the king's [doorkeeper] was killed [as well] as his lady cook and his lady brewer.

"[The jaw] was carefully removed from the ant heap, and presented [to] the new king; after which it was handed to the king's tailor who covered it with beads worked in patterns" (66-67).

The worst part of this ceremony was not the preservation of the jaw that was presented to the head widow, rather it was the fact that Mutesa had decreed that all his brothers should be imprisoned. He did this to stop any fighting over the succession.

The missionaries rejoiced that through their influence and the effect of Christianity, Mwanga's brothers were imprisoned rather than killed. Held in high esteem, the missionaries were soon in the grip of a corrosive routine. They provided medicine for the sick, settled quarrels, taught people to read, built chapels, fashioned each Christian community into an effective organization—and kept busy oiling the wheels of their bureaucracy.

Busy with his sixteen hours of grueling routine each day

colorful though some of it was, George Pilkington's ardent enthusiasm gradually began to cool. Having forgotten that Paul had warned the Galatians: "Let us not be weary in well doing: for in due season we shall reap, if we faint not" (6:9), his prayer life gradually slackened. He even began to skip the missionary prayer meetings.

In the midst of this ho-hum period, Musa Yubauanda, a convert who had chosen the name *Musa* (Moses) after his baptism in order to indicate his enthusiasm for the Lord, approached the missionaries. "You are not teachers of Christianity," he stormed, his brown eyes flashing angrily. "You are merely white administrators. I'm going to seek peace with God elsewhere!"

Stung by this accusation, Pilkington remembered how he had lectured the boys at Worcester Lodge. A key sentence he had used burned in his heart: "[It is useless] to tie fruit on a fruitless tree—the nature of the tree must be changed." *Could it be that he was now trying to tie fruit on a fruitless tree?*

Humbled by memories of the zeal he once had, Pilkington decided to go to the island of Kome, a few miles southeast of Port Alice on Lake Victoria, and be alone with the Lord. While relating to Mannix what had happened to Pilkington, Arthur Fisher was so overcome he replied with tears in his eyes: "When he returned to us, God had answered his prayers and the Holy Ghost had descended on him as truly as it ever did on the apostles" (Hunter and Mannix 72).

While speaking to a gathering of students in Liverpool, Pilkington related his experience on the island of Kome: "If it had not been that God enabled me, after three years in the mission field to accept by faith the gift of the Holy Spirit, I should have given up the work. I could not have gone on as I was then.

"A book by David, the Tamil evangelist, showed me that my life was not right, that I had not the power of the Holy Ghost. *I had consecreted myself hundreds of times, but I had not accepted God's gift*" (Battersly, n.p.).

Baskerville, a missionary to Uganda, wrote about Pilkington's experience: "Pilkington got back yesterday from

Kome about 5:30. . . . he told us how he had definitely, while away, received the Baptism of the Holy Ghost, and manifestations of his power had followed. . . .

"One man, a native of Kome stood up and said, 'You see me a native born, not of Baganda, not a native of Kome, do not call me any more by my old name, *for I have been born anew*'" (225).

Evangelistic fervor spread. Even the *katikiro* was touched and wrote his testimony, and Musa came back to the Christian faith.

Pilkington's pause on the island of Kome and his infilling with the Holy Spirit, had completely altered the vision and the power of the Church of Uganda.

Can you answer?
1. How did Julian the Apostate try to destroy Christians?
2. How did England finally get Mutesa's letter asking for missionaries?
3. What do the words *kabaka* and *katikiro* mean?
4. Who was George Pilkington?
5. Why did some of the Baganda learn to read upside down?
6. Had Pilkington ever consecrated his life before he was empowered by the Holy Spirit?
7. What did Pilkington do to receive the infilling of the Holy Spirit? What was the evidence that he had received the baptism of the Holy Spirit?

3

Who Is the Holy Spirit?

Strangely, those who spew filthy four-letter words and take the Lord's name in vain seldom if ever take the Holy Spirit's name in vain. This is amazing.

It would seem that if without a tinge of conscience, they ignore the explicit commandment: "You shall not misuse the name of the Lord your God, for the Lord will not hold anyone guiltless who misuses his name" (Exod. 20:7, NIV), they would also ignore Jesus' warning: "But whosoever blasphemes against the Holy Spirit will never be forgiven" (Mark 3:29, NIV). But they do not. Why?

Undoubtedly it is because they are *aware* of the Holy Spirit!

The Holy Spirit cannot be ignored. All classes of people are aware of him. This fact is illustrated again and again. I first became acutely aware of the Holy Spirit when I was seven or eight.

While sitting on the platform in the big Tabernacle at Anderson Camp Meeting, I watched a group of people during the invitation. Noticing their downcast eyes, long faces, and tears, I asked Ruth Fisher (later Ruth Murray) for an explanation.

"Oh," said she, "they're under *conviction*." Later, I learned, that Ruth's explanation meant that the Holy Spirit was striving with them.

In this fashion I, *a child*, became aware of the Holy Spirit.

Natives of the Prussian city of Konigsberg could set their watches by the movements of Immanuel Kant. The tiny bachelor was so methodical he started his evening stroll along what is still known as "The Philosopher's Walk" at exactly three-thirty P.M. During a rain, his servant shuffled ahead and protected him with an umbrella.

Kant was particular about his health, and so when he walked outside he never said a word; for he believed that if he breathed through his mouth he would get sick. Also, he attached his stockings to springs in his pockets so that they always stayed up and kept his legs warm.

As the outstanding philosopher of the eighteenth century, he had immense influence over his contemporaries—and he is still considered one of the greatest philosophers who ever lived.

Raised in a Pietist home, Kant was a God-fearing man.

Did the Holy Spirit influence Immanuel Kant? Certainly! Who can fail to be moved by his line that Beethoven loved to quote: "I am overwhelmed by two things—the starry heavens above [and] the moral law within."

Who is it that pricks our conscience when we violate "the moral law within?" The Holy Spirit! Who is it that encourages us when we face depression? The Holy Spirit! Who is it that points out new paths and urges us to follow them? The Holy Spirit! Who is it that leads the way to the wounded hands of Christ? The Holy Spirit!

In this manner even a *profound philosopher* like Immanuel Kant is made aware of the Holy Spirit.

In Acts 8 we learn about another type of person who became aware of the power of the Holy Spirit. His name was Simon. Simon had "practiced sorcery" (v. 9, NIV). After witnessing the way Peter and John laid hands on the Samaritans and how the Samaritans received the Holy Spirit, he realized at once the value of the Holy Spirit, and made a blasphemous request. Here's his story as recorded by J. B.

Phillips in verses 18 and 19: Without asking how he might *personally* receive the Holy Spirit, Simon offered Peter and John money and said:

"Give me this power too, so that if I were to put my hands on anyone he could receive the Holy Spirit."

In answer to this astonishing request, Peter answered: "To hell with you and your money![1] How dare you think you could buy the gift of God. All you can do now is to repent of this wickedness of yours and pray earnestly to God that the evil intention of your heart may be forgiven. For I can see inside you, and I see a man with bitter jealousy and bound with his own sin!" (vv. 20-21).

This incident illustrates how evil people, even a *sorcerer*, acknowledge the presence of the Holy Spirit.

But what about the illiterate? Could an illiterate who had never heard of Jesus be aware of the "moral law" impressed in the minds of the dispossessed? The answer to those questions comes thundering back to us when we consider the plight of illiterate slaves working from sunup to sundown in the Mississippi Delta. Those slaves have provided us with an immense treasure in the form of spirituals.

Here are the words of one of them as composed by unknown slaves as they sweated in the hot sun out in the fields. To a heart-searching tune they sang:

> There is a balm in Gilead
> to make the wounded whole;
> There is a balm in Gilead
> to heal the sin-sick soul.
> Sometimes I feel discouraged,
> And think my work's in vain,
> But then the Holy Spirit
> revives my soul again.

Having seen that *all types* of people, *literate* and *illiterate*, are aware of the Holy Spirit, let us now consider the various names he has been called in both the Old and New Testaments. Curiously, Jesus Christ, the Second Person in the

Trinity, is known throughout the New Testament by only one name: *Jesus Christ*. (In addition, of course, he is referred to or addressed as Rabbi, Teacher, Savior, and so on.) But the name of the Holy Spirit, the Third Person in the Trinity, has many official names.

According to J. E. Cummings, the Holy Spirit is referred to in 261 passages in the New Testament and 86 passages in the Old Testament (50-52).

As we consider these names, they, like the names in Dickens or Harriet Beecher Stowe's characters, tend to indicate his mission, personality, nativity—and power.

Doctor John F. Walvoord has done us a favor by pointing out eleven occasions in which the name of the Holy Spirit is linked to the First Person of the Trinity: God the Father and five times the Holy Spirit is linked to the Second Person of the Trinity: God the Son (10). Here they are with emphasis on the person of the Trinity indicated:

(1) Spirit of *God* (Gen. 1:2; Matt. 3:16); (2) Spirit of the *Lord* (Luke 4:18); (3) Spirit of *our God* (1 Cor. 6:11); (4) *his spirit* (Num. 11:29); (5) Spirit of *the Lord* (Jehovah)(Judges 3:10); (6) *thy spirit* (Psalm 139:7); (7) Spirit of the *Lord God* (Isa. 61:1); (8) Spirit of *your Father* (Matt. 10:20); (9) Spirit of the *Living God* (2 Cor. 3:3); (10) *My spirit* (Gen. 6:3); (11) Spirit of *him* (Romans 8:11).

The five references that link the Holy Spirit to Jesus Christ are as follows:

(1) Spirit of *Christ* (Romans 8:9; 1 Peter 1:11); (2) Spirit of *Jesus Christ* (Phil. 1:19); (3) Spirit of *Jesus* (Acts 16:7); (4) Spirit of *his Son* (Gal. 4:6); (5) Spirit of *the Lord* (Acts 5:9; 8:39).

Many argue that the Holy Spirit is *merely* a force; and so they refer to him as *it*. This is incorrect. Various passages clearly indicate that the Holy Spirit is a person along with miscellaneous facets of his personality. This has been done in the same manner in which the personality of God and Jesus Christ are indicated.

For example, Paul stated that the Holy Spirit can be grieved. "*Grieve* not the holy Spirit of God," he exhorted (Eph. 4:30).

Paul also prayed: "That the God of our Lord Jesus Christ, the Father of glory, may give unto you the *spirit of wisdom*" (Eph. 1:17). Being wise, the Holy Spirit knows when to strive with men and women and when to leave them alone. The Spirit also knows when to open and close doors for workers in the Kingdom.

When Jesus sent the Seventy out to evangelize, he gave them clear instructions: "But when you enter a town and are not welcomed, go into the streets and say, 'Even the dust of your town that sticks to our feet we wipe off against you' " (Luke 10:11, NIV). That the Holy Spirit limits his striving with women and men is indicated in Genesis 6:3—"And the Lord said, My spirit shall not always *strive* with man."

The Apostle Paul, perhaps because of his Damascus experience, before which he had "kick[ed] against the pricks" (Acts 9:5) was so acutely aware of this characteristic of the Holy Spirit he referred to it in colorful language in his very first canonical letter: "Do not *put out the Spirit's fire*" (1 Thess. 5:19, NIV).

Another characteristic is that the Holy Spirit is adept at *opening* and *closing* doors. In his Acts of the Apostles, Luke explained how Paul and his helpers faced both a closed door and then an opened door.

"When they came to the border of Mysia, they tried to enter Bithynia, but the Spirit of Jesus would not allow them to" (16:7, NIV). Realizing that the Holy Spirit had closed this door, they went on to Troas; and there "during the night Paul had a vision of a man of Macedonia standing and begging him, 'Come over to Macedonia and help us' " (v. 9, NIV).

Impressed by this opened door, Paul and his helpers went to Philippi and ended up in jail! But even though the jailor had them "severely flogged," and ordered "that they be guarded carefully" and someone "put them in the inner cell and fastened their feet in the stocks" (vv. 23-24, NIV), they were so confident that they had been led by the Holy Spirit that they prayed and sang hymns to God.

The situation seemed impossible; but, as we know, a congregation was started in Philippi; and later when Paul was suffering in prison, this congregation sent gifts to him. Thankfully, he responded: "I have received full payment and even more; I am amply supplied, now that I have received from Epaphroditus the gifts you sent" (Phil. 4:18, NIV).

One work of the Holy Spirit is seldom considered. This is the work in creation. Inspired by the Lord to write the Book of Genesis, Moses was led to credit the Holy Spirit for his part in this work. In unmistakable terms he wrote:

> The earth was without form, and void; and darkness was on the face of the deep. And the *Spirit of God* moved upon the face of the waters (Gen. 2:1).

Expanding on this theme, Walvoord has suggested that not only was the Holy Spirit a participant in creation, but that the Spirit *continues* as a participant in the life of creation. To bolster his suggestion, he quoted John Owen: "The [Hebrew word] moved [*merachepheth*] signified a gentle motion, like that of a dove over its nest, to communicate vital heat to its eggs, or to cherish its young. Without him, all was a dead sea; a rude in form chaos; a confused heap covered with darkness: but by the moving of the *Spirit* of God upon it, he communicated a quickening prolific virtue. The principles of all those kind of forms of things, which in an unconceivable variety compose its host and ornament, were communicated to it."[2]

Walvoord further sought to strengthen his suggestion that the Holy Spirit continues activity in nature by quoting Job 26:13—"By his spirit he hath garnished the heavens; his hand hath formed the crooked serpent."

According to some commentators, *the crooked serpent* is "the north constellation of stars." Owen thought it referred to the "Milky Way." No one, of course, can pinpoint the exact meaning of Job's statement; but when we consider the vastness of the billions of galaxies, we have to agree that they are controlled by an intelligence far beyond our comprehension.

As imaginative as these thoughts may be, we have the very definite statement in Psalm 104:30 that the Holy Spirit is in charge of creation. There, the unknown author wrote: "Thou sendest forth thy spirit, they are created: and thou renewest the face of the earth."

In chapter 11, titled "The Holy Spirit's Ministry," we will write more about the functions of the Holy Spirit and how his labors can affect our lives. But right now we are faced with a question that is on the lips of many. That question is this: We've heard about the Holy Spirit's duties and personality, *but who is the Holy Spirit, and where did the Holy Spirit come from?*

Conservative Christianity believes in the Trinity, which is God the *Father*; God the *Son*; and God the *Holy Spirit*. But many will be shocked to learn that the word *Trinity*, in addition to the words *Rapture* and *Millennium*, are not found in the Bible.

The expression *Trinity* is an anglicized form of the Latin *trinitas*. That root word *trinitas* was first used by Tertullian, an attorney who was not born until around A. D. 155! In addition, many lay people will be shocked to discover that one of the most quoted texts in the Bible used to prove the Trinity, is a disputed text. That passage reads: "For there are three that bear record in heaven, the Father, the Word, and the Holy Ghost: and these three are one" (1 John 5:7).

A footnote in the NIV, states that neither verse 7 nor 8 of that contested passage is found "in any Greek manuscript before the sixteenth century." That does not mean, however, that the doctrine of the Trinity is not true!

But first, let us pause and scan the battles that have raged over the Trinity.

Those who deny the three-part Godhead use their nimble fingers to turn to proof texts to abolish Trinitarians.

Here are three of their favorite passages: An oft-quoted one is from Deuteronomy 6:4. Jesus himself quoted this passage in Mark 12:29. "Jesus answered him, the first of all commandments is, *Hear, O Israel; The Lord our God is one Lord*." Another is found in Zechariah 14:9: "The Lord shall be king over all the earth: in that day shall there be *one* Lord, and his name *one*."

In opposition to these passages, Trinitarians also have a long series of arguments and proof texts: "And God said, let *us* make man in *our* image" (Gen. 1:28). "The Lord God said, Behold, the man is become as one of *us*" (Gen. 3:22). "The Lord appeared unto [Abraham] in the plains of Mamre" (Gen. 18:1). Notice, at this point the word *Lord* is singular. But in the next three verses we read: "He lifted up his eyes and looked and, lo, *three* men stood by him: and when he saw *them*, he ran to meet *them* . . . and said My *Lord*."

Next, in verse twenty-two we get another hint about the three-in-one Godhead: "The men turned their faces from thence, and went toward Sodom: but Abraham stood yet before the *Lord*."

These passages in chapter 18 leave room for debate. Nevertheless, they bristle with at least a hint of the Trinity.

Isaiah's vision in the sixth chapter also contains a hint of the Trinity. "I saw the *Lord* sitting upon a throne" (v. 1). "And *one* [seraphim] cried unto another, and said Holy, holy, holy is the Lord of hosts: the whole earth is full of his glory" (v. 3).

Then in verses six and seven we read "Then flew *one* of the seraphims unto me, having a live coal in his hand, which he had taken with tongs from off the altar: And he laid it upon my mouth, and said, Lo, this hath touched thy lips; and thine iniquity is taken away, and thy sin purged."

In this chapter we see the *Lord*; *one* who praises the Lord; and *one* who cleanses from sin. In other words Isaiah saw each of the *three* principle manifestations of the Godhead.

In the New Testament numerous other passages support the doctrine of the Trinity:

"Go ye therefore, and teach all nations, baptizing them in the name of the *Father*, and of the *Son*, and of the *Holy Ghost*" (Matt. 28:19).

"Wherefore I give you to understand, that no man speaking by the *Spirit* of God calleth *Jesus* accursed: and that no man can say that *Jesus* is the *Lord*, but by the *Holy Ghost*" (1 Cor. 12:3).

In addition to these and similar passages we have the fact that all three persons of the Trinity were present at Jesus' baptism. "*Jesus* when he was baptized went up straightway out of the water: and, lo, the heavens were opened unto him, and he saw the *Spirit of God* descending like a dove, and lighting upon him: And lo a voice from heaven, saying, This is my beloved *Son*, in whom *I* am well pleased" (Matt. 3:16-17).

Many who lived in the early centuries of Christianity had keen minds and frequently used them to split hairs. One of the most notorious hair-splitters was Arius. Arius contended that "If the Father begat the Son, he that was begotten had a beginning of existence; and from this it is evident, that there was [a time] when the Son was not. It therefore . . . follows that he had his subsistence from nothing" (Douglas 67).

This idea, beloved by Jehovah's Witnesses, caused so much havoc that Constantine summoned what is now called the Council of Nicea in 325. This council of bishops met in Nicea, now Iznik in northwestern Turkey. The three hundred robed bishops hammered out the Nicene Creed, which declares in part:

> We believe in one God, the Father almighty, maker of heaven and earth, and of all things visible and invisible; and in one Lord Jesus Christ, the only-begotten Son of God, begotten from the Father before all ages, light from light, true God from true God, begotten, not made, of one substance with the Father, through whom all things

came into existence, who for us men and because of our salvation, came down from heaven, and was incarnate from the Holy Spirit of the Virgin Mary, and became man. . . .

And [we believe in] the Holy Spirit, the Lord and the life-giver, *who proceeds from the Father, who with the Father and the Son is together is worshiped and together glorified, who spoke through the prophets* (Encyclopedia Britannica).

This creed did not settle the debate over the Trinity, for the hair-splitters kept busy. During the debate no one was more vocal than Athanasius. This tiny shadow of a man disputed Arius and contended that Jesus was indeed the *eternal* Son of God.

So tenacious was he that his name has become a symbol of indomitability. In his struggles, Athanasius survived five exiles and remained in hiding for the best part of seventeen years. But today, in his honor, we have the Athanasian Creed which, though named after him, was written by others centuries after his death.

The Athanasian Creed states the reality of the Trinity in such a precise way that it is accepted by both Catholic and most Protestant persuasions. Originated in Latin, the Athanasian Creed declares:

We worship one God in Trinity, and Trinity in Unity; neither confounding the persons, nor dividing the substance. For there is one person of the Father; another of the Son; and another of the Holy Ghost. But the Godhead of the Father, and of the Son, and of the Holy Ghost is all one; the Glory equal, the Majesty coeternal. . . . So the Father is God: the Son is God: and the Holy Ghost is God. And yet there are not three gods but one God. The Father is made of none: neither created nor begotten. The Son is of the Father alone; not made, nor created, nor begotten: but proceeding. . . . And in this Trinity none is afore, or after another; nor is greater, or less than another. But the whole three persons are coeternal, and coequal. So that in all things, as aforesaid: the Unity in Trinity and the Trinity in Unity, is to be worshiped.

In the next chapter we will discuss the work of the Holy Spirit in the Old Testament.

Can you answer?
1. Why don't people swear by the Holy Spirit?
2. Name two things that overwhelmed Immanuel Kant.
3. Why did Peter denounce Simon the Sorcerer?
4. Is the Holy Spirit referred to by more than one name?
5. Does Scripture ever link the Holy Spirit with God and Christ?
6. Is the Holy Spirit a person?
7. Who was Athanasius?

4

The Holy Spirit in the Old Testament

Although referred to more than three times as often in the New Testament as in the Old Testament, nevertheless the Holy Spirit's presence, work, and personality in the Old Testament is extremely convincing.

Genesis 1:2 could not be more specific: "And the *Spirit of God* moved upon the face of the waters."

After the *New Testament Pentecost* when the Twelve went out to evangelize the world, they faced hostilities everywhere. "Mud-and-Blood" (Tiberius Caesar) was on the throne at Rome; Saul of Tarsus was "still breathing out murderous threats against the Lord's disciples" (Acts 9:1, NIV); and the Jews were passionately hostile toward them. After all, the Followers of the Way had accepted Jesus as the Messiah even though he hadn't tossed the Romans into the sea; and, almost as bad, the followers of Jesus often ate with Gentiles!

As the Twelve went from place to place, their only scroll of reference was the Septuagint—the Greek translation of the Old Testament.

They had with them, however, vibrant memories of the words of Jesus and his appearances after his death and burial. One can easily imagine Peter arising in a synagogue and with a scroll in his hands, outlining his experiences with Jesus, and showing how Isaiah had predicted his coming in chapter 53.

Likewise Thomas had a great story. I can almost hear him

say, "I was a doubter. I just could not believe that Jesus had survived the tomb. But then he came into the room where I was sitting with the others; and not only did he show me his wounds, but he even asked me to put my finger and then my hand into the prints in his hands and the gash in his side. On that occasion, an occasion I can't forget, I exclaimed: 'My Lord and my God.' That experience shaped my life!"

The stories of the Twelve were both gripping and spellbinding. Ah, but they had an additional power. Each remembered how on the last day of the Feast of Tabernacles Jesus had said, "Whosoever believes in me, as the Scripture has said, streams of living water, will flow from within him" (John 7:38, NIV).

Some seventy years later, John explained Jesus' statement: "By this he meant the Spirit, whom those who believed in him were later to receive" (v. 39, NIV). He wrote this with a firm hand in spite of the fact that all the other apostles had been martyred and he had narrowly survived when he was plunged into a cauldron of boiling oil by the order of Christ-hating Domitian.

John's explanation came from memory, experience—and the inspiration of the Holy Spirit.

Because of the "living water" flowing out of their lives, both John and the others were astounded by what they could do. In addition, the apostles never could forget how that in the Upper Room, Jesus had, in a calm and yet matter-of-fact voice, said, "But I tell you the truth: It is for your good that I am going away. Unless I go away, the Counselor will not come to you; but if I go, I will send him to you" (John 16:7, NIV).

Were Jesus' statements accurate? Acts 17:6 answers that question: "And when [lewd fellows of the baser sort] found them not, they drew Jason and certain of the brethren unto the rulers of the city, crying, *These that have turned the world upside down are come here also.*"

Those who lived in Old Testament times were not as well equipped as Peter, James, and John; for they had not been ministered to by Jesus, had not seen Jesus raise people from the dead, feed the multitude with a few loaves and fishes; nor had they seen the empty tomb, the wounds in his hands and feet, or even witnessed the Ascension.

Even so, they had been directed by the entire Trinity!

Notice how the Holy Spirit ministered in Old Testament times by helping people to be *creative*.

The Book of Job is an example. The author or authors of this masterpiece, written between 600 and 400 B.C., and maybe earlier, did not have access to the books that crowd our libraries. Nonetheless, the writers wrote with accuracy about events that were to come to pass hundreds of years later.

Replying to a "comforter," Job said: "Behold now, I have ordered my cause; I know that I shall be *justified*" (13:18). (His word *justified* electrified Luther two millennia later!)

In response to his own question, "If a man die, shall he live again?" (14:14), Job answered: "For I know that my *redeemer* liveth, and that he shall stand at the latter day upon the earth: and though after my skin worms destroy this body, yet *in my flesh shall I see God*" (19:25-26).

How could the author(s?) of Job write about the "redeemer," "justification," "the Second Coming," and immortality? By the *creative* power of the Holy Spirit!

Dazzled by the Book of Job, Victor Hugo exclaimed: "The Book of Job is perhaps the greatest masterpiece of the human mind."

The only solution to the way he was enabled to produce this masterpiece is that he was inspired by the Holy Spirit.

We'll now swing over to the Pentateuch, the first five books in our modern Bibles. No one can be dogmatic about the date of its composition or the main author or number of authors who wrote, contributed to, edited, or complied it.

Nonetheless, we can be dogmatic about one fact; and that fact is that the influence of the Holy Spirit saturates every verse, just as the Holy Spirit saturates all the 31,173 verses of the Bible.

Again, while still thinking of the creativity of the Holy Spirit, we are faced with the thoroughly amazing literary quality of both the Old and the New Testaments. Many successful reporters like to recall that after they had turned in their first carefully scripted article, their editor barked, "Too wordy. Read the first chapter of Genesis!"

No evangelical doubts that John, author of the Fourth Gospel, had experienced the Holy Spirit baptism. In addition, he had been the closest one to Jesus in the Upper Room when Jesus told them that they would do "greater works" than he had done. Also, he had been with Jesus during his final hours in Gethsemane; he alone among the Twelve had lingered at the foot of the Cross while Jesus was dying; and Jesus had entrusted the care of his mother to him. What was the opening sentence in the Gospel that bears his name? It is the same opening that was used in Genesis 1:1—*"In the beginning."*

In Genesis 3:15 we read the first veiled reference to Jesus Christ. The author dipped his pen almost a millennium before Jesus was born in Bethlehem and wrote: "I will put enmity between thee and the woman, and between thy seed and her seed; it shall bruise thy head, and thou shalt bruise his heel." That is undoubtedly difficult for many to understand in our time, especially if they don't have a good biblical background. Phillips Brook's sermon titled: "The Giant with the Wounded Heel" is helpful at this point. Brooks pointed out that "man is subject to the poisonous fangs of sin" but through Christ one can crush sin if one is so determined.

As we continue through the Old Testament we are faced again and again with sparkling literary gems that are alloyed with prophecy concerning the coming Messiah and were planted in the hearts of the authors by the Holy Spirit.

A cynic was quoted as having said, "Man gained the ability to speak to the entire world at the approximate moment when he had nothing worthwhile to say." That, however, was not a fact with the prophets, for they were inspired by the Holy Spirit. Referring to them, Peter wrote: "Above all, you must understand that no prophecy of Scripture came about by the prophet's own interpretation. For prophecy never had its origin in the will of man, but men *spoke* from *God* as they were carried along by the *Holy Spirit*" (2 Peter 1:20-21, NIV).

The Lord's prophets were held in high esteem and when their words were copied, the author's words, like other words in the Bible, were considered sacred. Geddes MacGregor in his book *The Bible in the Making* has pointed out how careful each scribe had to be:

"The scroll of the Law for use in a synagogue had to be fastened . . . with strings made from "clean" animals. . . . Lines had to be drawn before the writing was done, and if a scribe inadvertently wrote more than three words without first lining his copy, the whole thing was rendered worthless. He had to see that the space of a thread lay between each two consecutive letters that he wrote, and he was not allowed to write a single letter from memory, without first looking at the approved text from which he was making his copy. He had to see that he never began the sacred name of God with a pen newly dipped in ink, lest he spatter. Throughout the whole of his work, the scribe was required to sit in full Jewish dress, and he was forbidden to speak to anyone, even a king" (22).

Realizing the worshipful reverence in which the people held their sacred poets, prophets, and lawgivers, we will repeat some of their prized statements—especially those that refer to the coming of the Messiah. We have quoted them in chronological order.

> He is the one who will build a house for my Name, and I will establish the throne of his kingdom forever. I will be his father and he will be my son (2 Sam. 7:13-14, NIV, written between 1050-1000 during the reigns of Saul and David).

> I have made a covenant with my chosen, I have sworn unto David my servant. Thy seed will I

establish for ever, and build up thy throne to all generations (Ps. 89:3-4, written by a believer probably during the reign of David).

My God, my God, why hast thou forsaken me? why art thou so far from me, and from the words of my roaring? (Ps. 22:1).

Often called the Psalm of the Cross, this psalm of David was quoted by Jesus as he was dying between the thieves on Golgotha.

Isaiah wrote so much about the coming Messiah that his prophecies have been referred to as the Gospel of Isaiah. Our first quote is from Isaiah's famous sixth chapter written between 740 and 700 B.C.

"In the year that king Uzziah died, I saw also the Lord sitting upon a throne, . . . and his train filled the temple" (v. 1).

From there we skip to the seventh chapter and the fourteenth verse:

"Therefore the Lord himself shall give you a sign: The virgin will be with child and will give birth to a son, and will call him Immanuel" (NIV).

Now we must pause for a moment at the fifty-third chapter:

"Who hath believed our report? and to whom is the arm of the Lord revealed? For he shall grow up before him as a tender plant, and as a root out of a dry ground: he hath no form nor comeliness; and when we shall see him there is no beauty that we should desire him. He is despised and rejected of men; a man of sorrows, and acquainted with grief" (vv. 1-3).

But even though crimson threads reach through and "bind" the entire Old Testament, those thirty-nine books had other functions in addition to predicting the coming of the Messiah. One of those operations was to record the reactions of penitents whose consciences had been pricked by the Holy Spirit. None of us can ever forget the cry of King Saul when he was confronted by David whom he had sought to kill:

"I have played the fool, and have erred exceedingly" (1 Sam. 26:21).

And who can forget the psalm of David in which he expressed his contrition over his adultery and his murder of Uriah the Hittite? Inspired by the Holy Spirit, this psalm quivers with remorse and tenderness. In our time it might have won a Nobel prize. Shakespeare could not have equaled it. Listen!

"Have mercy on me, O God, according to thy loving-kindness. . . . Wash me thoroughly from mine iniquity. . . . For I acknowledge my transgressions: and my sin is ever before me. Against thee, thee only, have I sinned, and done this evil in thy sight. . . . Behold I was shapen in iniquity; and in sin did my mother conceive me. . . . Purge me with hyssop, and I shall be clean: wash me, and I shall be whiter than snow. . . . Deliver me from bloodguiltiness, O God, thou God of my salvation: and my tongue shall sing aloud of thy righteousness. O Lord open thou my lips; and my mouth shall show forth thy praise (from Ps. 51:1-14).

Two other facets of the work of the Holy Spirit demonstrated in the Old Testament are that the Spirit provides followers with both *courage*—and *power*. Take a glance at Deborah, the judge, prophetess, and wife who ruled an area between Ramah and Bethel in Ephraim.

For twenty years the Israelites had been oppressed by the Canaanites; but they were so paralyzed with fear that they were afraid even to try and shake off their yoke; for Sisera, their enemy's commander, had "nine hundred chariots of iron" (Judg. 4:3).

Deborah, however, hurried out from under her palm tree where she held court and challenged Barak. "Go," she said, "take with you ten thousand men of Naphtali and Zebulun and lead the way to Mount Tabor. I will lure Sisera . . . with his chariots and his troops to the Kishon River and give him into your hands.

"Barak replied, 'If you go with me I will go; but if you don't go with me, I won't go' " (Judges 4:6-8, NIV).

Deborah replied: "Very well, I will go with you. But because of the way you are going about this, the honor will not be yours, for the Lord will hand over Sisera to a woman" (v. 9, NIV).

The battle took place along the right bank of the river Kishon. As they fought, they were inundated by such heavy rains that Sisera's nine hundred iron chariots floundered in the mud and "the river of Kishon swept them away" (5:21). Sisera's army was hacked to pieces. He, himself, was put to death by a woman who pounded a stake through his temples.

Overjoyed, the people celebrated by triumphantly singing:

"The stars in their courses fought against Sisera"
(5:20).

Because of the guidance of the Holy Spirit, the Children of Israel were freed. Barak was honored by being included in the faith gallery of Hebrews 11, and the area where Deborah ruled was renamed the "Palm of Deborah." In our time, thinking of her, we name our daughters Deborah!

The power of the entire Trinity in the Old Testament was summed up by Job. In the midst of his troubles, after having lost all his children, together with his wealth; and after being stricken with boils, he continued to smile and certify his faith. "Though he slay me," he affirmed, "yet will I trust him" (Job 13:15).

The entire Bible is, and will continue to be, the greatest book ever written. Thoroughly inspired, it contains the loftiest thoughts, the greatest and most creative poetry and prose, and it points to life-changing power.

We must never forget that the Holy Spirit was extremely active in Old Testament times.

Can you answer?
1. Where was the coming of Christ first mentioned in the Old Testament? Who inspired the writer to write it?
2. What did Victor Hugo say about the book of Job?
3. How did Job know that his "redeemer" was alive?
4. Did Job believe in immortality?
5. What did the seraphim place on the lips of Isaiah?
6. How did Deborah gain a victory over Sisera?
7. What book did the Twelve have to rely on when they began to evangelize the world?

5

Old Testament Pentecost

Backgrounded by the Law of Moses—"I am a Pharisee, the son of a Pharisee" (Acts 23:6)—Paul wrote to the Galatians: "Wherefore the law [of Moses] was our schoolmaster to bring us unto Christ, that we might be justified by faith" (3:24). This being so, we can get brilliant streams of new light and understanding of New Testament Pentecost by studying Old Testament Pentecost.

Strangely, the feast, which we are calling Old Testament Pentecost, did not begin as Old Testament Pentecost! At its beginning, it was known at the Feast of Harvest (Exod. 23:16); next as the Feast of Weeks (Exod. 34:22); and then as Pentecost. It acquired this final name from Greek-speaking Jews because in spite of its various titles, it was to be celebrated on the *fiftieth* day after the Passover.

The Greek word for fiftieth is *pentecostos*.

It is exhilarating for Christians to realize that the feast of Pentecost, regardless of its name, was always associated with, and was, indeed, a continuation of the Passover.

Those early names, however, are vital; for, as we consider them, we soon realize that each one, along with the reason for each one, points more and more directly to the New Testament Pentecost, the birthday of the Church.

Because of this, our understanding of New Testament Pentecost will be greatly enhanced if we understand Old

Testament Pentecost and why it was considered a continuation of the Passover. We must, therefore, first pause and think about the earlier Passover feast.

Having resisted the nine plagues—frogs, contaminated water, lice, flies, and the others—with which the Lord had afflicted the Egyptians, Pharaoh still refused to release the Israelites. The Lord then instructed Moses on how the Israelites were to prepare for their final meal before their escape that would take place after the Angel of Death had taken the life of the eldest son in each Egyptian family.

Here is a synopsis of what Moses was to instruct the Israelites to do.

On the tenth of the month, each family was to secure a year-old lamb that was without blemish. This lamb was to be killed at twilight on the fourteenth day of that month, the first month in their calendar. (Before the Exile, this month was called *Abib* (month of the ears) for it was at that time that barley began to green. After the Exile it was renamed *Nisan* (flowering). Nisan falls between March and April.) Each family was then to take some of the [lamb's] blood and put it on the sides and tops of the doorframes of the houses where they [would] eat the lambs. . . . This is how you are to eat it: with your cloak tucked into your belt, your sandals on your feet and your staff in your hand. Eat it in *haste*; it is the *Lord's Passover* (Exod. 12:7, 11, NIV).

That night at "about" midnight, the Angel of Death swooped over Egypt and snuffed out the life of each firstborn, including that of the oldest son of Pharaoh, the firstborn of each slave girl, and even the initial offspring of the cattle.

There was weeping and wailing all through that ancient nation watered by the Nile. Even so, the Lord had promised: "But among the Israelites not a dog will bark at any man or animal. Then you will know that the Lord makes a distinction between Egypt and Israel" (Exodus 11:7, NIV).

That night, after eating their roasted lambs and bitter

herbs, the Israelites escaped the clenched fist of Pharaoh. Since the Lord wanted them to remember the night during which the Angel of Death *passed over* the houses marked with blood, he instituted the Passover.

During this feast, they were to eat a roasted lamb along with unleavened bread "from the evening of the fourteenth day until the evening of the twenty-first day" (Exodus 12:18, NIV). That they were to eat *unleavened* bread was emphasized in the next verse. *"For seven days no yeast is to be found in your houses. And whoever eats anything with yeast in it must be cut off from the community of Israel, whether he is an alien or native born.* Eat nothing made with *yeast.* Wherever you live, you must eat *unleavened* bread" (Exodus 12:19-20, NIV).

The reason for the unleavened bread was to remind them of the haste in which they left Egypt. This detail was so important that the word *unleavened* is mentioned in Genesis, Exodus, Leviticus, and Numbers eighteen times in the Revised Standard Version!

In addition to the unleavened bread that partakers of the Passover must eat, there are "bitter herbs" that must also be eaten. Moses was commanded to instruct them to do this in Exodus 12:8, NIV—"That same night they are to eat the meat roasted over the fire, along with *bitter herbs*, and bread made without yeast."

In those initial days the bitter herbs included lettuce, endive, parsley, and others. In modern times, horseradish is also used. The bitter herbs remind the partakers of the bitter lives that they endurd during slavery.

The Laws of Moses are still sternly obeyed by orthodox Jews who are unswervingly kosher. This fact was impressed on me when I went to Israel on a trip sponsored by the Israeli government for Christian journalists.

Since we flew by El Al, Jewish orthodoxy was clearly evident. Numerous passengers wore phylacteries, one on their foreheads and one on the left arm. The black case, made from cardboard or the skin of a "clean" animal, was secured between their eyes with straps. It contained four passages from the Old Testament: Exod. 13:1-10, 11-16; and

Deut. 6:4-9; 11:13-21. The knot that secured the head phylactery was tied at the back of the neck in the form of the Hebrew letter *daleth*.

Each text was written in a meticulous style and without correction or erasure. The phylactery on the left arm contains the same texts. It is attached to the arm by a strap wound seven times around the arm and then secured to the middle and fourth fingers.

I learned on this flight that if I put cream in my coffee I was not to eat meat until six hours later. Why? Because Moses had taught: "Do not cook a young goat in its mother's milk" (Exod. 23:19; and 34:26, NIV).

Altogether, an orthodox Jewish housewife is required to observe hundreds of laws. For example, meat must *never* be cooked in butter. That would violate Exod. 23:19.

Food was never to be prepared *on* the Sabbath; but food could be prepared during the week that would be eaten on the Sabbath. Such food, however, should be prepared with the *express* purpose of eating it on the Sabbath. Otherwise, the previously prepared food could not be eaten. Edersheim has given us a colorful example indicating the way laws could be rationalized:

> If a hen laid on the Sabbath, the egg was forbidden because evidently it couldn't have been destined on a weekday for eating, since it had not yet laid, and did not exist; while if the hen had not been kept for laying but for fattening, the egg might be eaten *as forming a part of the hen that had fallen off*! (787).

The harvest festival announced in Exodus 23:16 was celebrated by presenting an offering from their crops: "Celebrate the Feast of Harvest with the firstfruits of the crops you sow in your field" (NIV).

The date of this feast was and is considered by Judaism to be extremely important. The rule is categorical: "From the day after the Sabbath, the day you brought the sheaf of the wave offering, count off *seven full* weeks. Count off fifty days after the seventh Sabbath, and then present an offering of *new* grain to the Lord" (Leviticus 23:15-16, NIV).

To pinpoint this date, we must also pinpoint the date of the "wave offering" that took place during the Passover. This offering, the waving of a sheaf of "the first ripe barley" before the Lord, took place *during* Passover on the sixteenth of Nisan.

This harvest festival later known as the Festival of Weeks was so called because it took place *after* the seventh week. In modern Judaism, each of the seven weeks is announced from Sabbath to Sabbath in the synagogue and a blessing is pronounced.

As the Children of Israel became established in the Promised Land, they began to celebrate the giving of the Law during this festival. In concentrating on the Ten Commandments presented to Moses by God and then relayed to the people, the rabbis have sifted every Scripture and every legend they could find in order to emphasize the importance of the event.

As a result of their studies, Jewish scholarship believes that the Lord handed the stones inscribed with the Law to Moses on a mountain in the Sinai Desert. This mountain is "at the head of the Red Sea, between the Gulf of Akaba and the Gulf of Suez, the two arms of that sea" (Greenstone 230). Today that mountain is called Jabal Musa (The Hill of Moses.) Its highest peak is labeled Sufsafe (the peak of the willow tree). It is 6,937 feet high.

Emphasizing the Torah (the Pentateuch), which contains the Law, rabbinic tradition has uncovered some curious traditions, many of which may have a spot of truth in them.

One rabbinic legend insists that "The Revelation at Mount Sinai was given in seventy languages, meaning all the vernaculars in vogue at that time" (230).

Another legend, a wild one, states that Israel was unwilling to accept the Torah and so "when the entire nation stood at the foot of Mount Sinai, God lifted up the mountain and held it over their heads like a basket, and said to them: 'If you accept the Torah it will be well with you; otherwise your grave will be under the mountain' whereupon the people cried: 'All that the Lord hath said we will do and be obedient' " (239).

Yet another legend suggests that: "the Revelation [the giving of the Law] took place in the wilderness [in order] to indicate that the Torah is free to all, even as the wilderness has no ownership" (240).

This Old Testament feast of Pentecost included not only an offering of their harvests, but animal sacrifices as well. They were to "Present a burnt offering of two young bulls, one ram and seven male lambs a year old as an aroma pleasing to the Lord. With each bull there is to be a grain offering of three-tenths of an ephah [5.8 gallons] of fine flour mixed with oil; with the ram two-tenths; and with each of the seven lambs, one-tenth."

Also, they were to "include one male goat to make atonement for you" (Num. 28:27-31, NIV).

The Old Testament Pentecost and the Passover differ in two main ways. One radical difference was that Passover was designed to underline the sufferings the Israelites had endured as slaves in Egypt. This was done by insisting that they eat bitter herbs.

In Old Testament Pentecost no one was required to eat bitter herbs.

Another radical difference was that whereas the people were required to eat *unleavened* bread at Passover, they were provided with *leavened* bread at the feast of Pentecost. Indeed, the joy of leavened bread was emphasized at Pentecost at the time of the wave offering.

Not only was the bread at Pentecost leavened, but there was *twice* as much! This was because this feast came at the time of the wheat harvest, and thus it was a time of joy. "In shape," Edersheim tells us, "[the loaves] were long and flat, and turned up either at the edges or the corners. . . . Each loaf was four handbreadths wide, seven feet long, and four fingers high. The dough would weigh about five pounds and three-quarters" (264-65).

Old Testament Pentecost, now referred to by Jews as *Shabout* was a popular feast. Josephus noted that it was attended by tens of thousands. There was much singing, large displays of flowers, both potted and cut, magnificent garlands of roses, flute playing, and reading romantic selections from the Book of Ruth.

The temple where the feast was celebrated had within it the atmosphere of a wedding. There were significant reasons for this joy:

> 1. The wheat harvest was in; and now those who had worked so hard to cultivate their fields could enjoy their prosperity and a period of rest.
> 2. Instead of having to eat unleavened bread and bitter herbs, they could eat bread that was alive with yeast and feel a sense of security and accomplishment.
> 3. Julius Greenstone has pointed out another reason for the intense joy the Israelites experience during this feast. "In the rabbinic *Aggada*, Passover is regarded as the time when *Israel* was *engaged* to God, and Shabuot [Pentecost] as *the* day of the *nuptials*. Just as the prospective bride counts the days between the engagement and the wedding, in her eagerness for the great day to arrive, so Israel counted the days in its yearning for the *complete* union with God (Greenstone 225).

During the last Pentecost before the Crucifixion, did the celebrants realize that at the next Pentecost, the Bride of Christ, the Church, was to be born? Undoubtedly they did not!

In the next chapter we will think about the price Jesus paid for his bride, his final courtship in his resurrected body before the Ascension—and the way the eleven disciples, especially the Big Fisherman, reacted in the midst of that courtship.

Can you answer?
1. What is the "schoolmaster" that points to Christ?
2. What was the *first* name of Old Testament Pentecost?
3. Why in later years was this feast called Pentecost?
4. What is the meaning of *Abib? Nisan?*
5. Why do Jews eat unleavened bread and bitter herbs at Passover? Name some of the bitter herbs.
6. Was the bread at Pentecost leavened or unleavened?
7. What is a phylactery?

6

The Rooster That Changed the World

Among the most famous birds that ever lived are the dove that alerted Noah to the fact that the flood was receding; the cackling geese that saved Rome; and the sea gulls that devoured the crickets that were destroying Mormon crops in 1848.

The *most* famous bird, however, was a rooster. This rooster changed the world by crowing in Jerusalem on April 7, A.D. 29. But to properly understand him—his bronze likeness tops many Catholic churches in Europe—we must return to the Upper Room.

As we view the Twelve crowded around Jesus in that room, two conclusions are forced upon us: (1) Even though they had spent three years with Jesus, they did not understand him. (2) although a new era was less than two months away, none of them really anticipated it. All of the Twelve were puzzled men.

Unlike the Ten Virgins, they didn't expect a wedding!

Since we lack space to study each of the Twelve as they fellowshipped with Jesus in the Upper Room, we will merely concentrate our remarks on Simon Peter, the one who always heads the list of apostles.

Simon's feelings must have been similar to those of the others. That evening, just after that "Last Supper," he unconsciously revealed one of his main defects during the foot-washing ceremony.

Let's move the camera for a closeup. As the candles flickered and the fragrance of roasted lamb, unleavened bread, and bitter herbs filled the air, Jesus left the place where he had been sitting next to John. Then he shed his outer garment and selected a towel. Here is what John remembered:

"After that he poured water into a basin and began to wash the disciples' feet, drying them with the towel that was wrapped around him. He came to Simon Peter who said to him, 'Lord, are you going to wash my feet?'

"Jesus replied, 'You do not realize now what I am doing, but later you will understand.' "

In answer to Jesus' statement, a shocked Peter almost exploded: " 'No, you will never wash my feet!' "

"Jesus answered, 'Unless I wash you, you have no part with me' " (13:5-8, NIV).

This prod got to Peter. Characteristically, he overreacted:

"Then Lord, not just my feet but my *hands* and *head* as well!" (v. 9).

Following the exit of Judas and Jesus' remark that "Where I'm going, you cannot follow now, but you will follow later," Peter blustered: "Lord, why can't I follow you now? *I will lay down my life for you*" (13:37, NIV). As strong as this statement was, Luke tells us that he also said: "I am ready to go with you to prison and to death" (Luke 22:33, NIV).

This second overreaction must have brought a smile to Jesus' lips, for he replied abruptly with a little humor mixed somewhat evenly with sternness: "Simon, Simon, Satan has asked to sift you as wheat. But I have prayed for you, Simon, that your faith may not fail. . . . I tell you, Peter, before the rooster crows today you will deny three times that you know me" (Luke 22:31, 33, NIV).

Was Peter embarrassed by these remarks? Probably not, for he was used to being both praised and rebuked by Jesus. No student of Simon Peter would choose to forget the occasion when Jesus was lavish with his praise: "Thou art

Peter, and upon this rock I will build my church; and the gates of hell shall not prevail against it" (Matt. 16:18); nor could he ever forget the stinging rebuke that Matthew placed in his gospel a mere five verses later: "Out of my sight, *Satan!* You are a stumbling block to me; you do not have in mind the things of God, but the things of men" (v. 23).

Later that evening, after Judas had gone out to complete his arrangements to betray Jesus, Jesus led the eleven down the steps and headed for the Garden of Gethsemane. Conscious of the fact that this was his last opportunity to speak at length with the eleven, Jesus gave them the incomparable words that begin with the statement: "Let not your hearts be troubled: ye believe in God, believe also in me. In my Father's house are many mansions: if it were not so, I would have told you. I go to prepare a place for you." That statement, the opening of the fourteenth chapter of John, continued on with one heart-lifting promise after another.

Where was Peter as Jesus led the group to the east side of the temple, then north by the slender and yet towering pinnacle where Satan had tempted him? The New Testament doesn't say. But it is reasonable to assume that he was as close to Jesus as his shadow.

The eleven continued northward by the wall of the temple and then turned east across the Kidron Valley with its tiny stream curving and bubbling on its way.

The Kidron Valley had many reminders of the past—reminders that were clearly outlined by the full paschal moon. Between the sloping banks there were the ancient tombs of Jehoshaphat, Absolam, Zechariah, and others, and because of the Passover season, these tombs had been given a fresh coat of whitewash as a stern warning.

The warning was so that pilgrims would not accidentally be defiled by touching one of them as they searched for a place to camp. Defilement, even accidental defilement, would exclude them from the Passover Feast.

Obvious also was the revered route that David had followed when he wrested Jerusalem from the Jebusites; and the traditional place where David had fled from his own son Absalom were clearly evident. These historical spots were places where visitors—especially wide-eyed children—loved to visit.

Somewhere on this, his final journey with the eleven before his crucifixion, Jesus pointed to a series of grapevines. "I am the true vine," he said, "and my Father is the gardener. He cuts off every branch in me that bears no fruit, while every branch that does bear fruit he prunes so that it will be even more fruitful. You are already clean because of the word I have spoken unto you. Remain in me and I will remain in you. No branch can bear fruit by itself; it must remain in the vine. Neither can you bear fruit unless you remain in me" (John 15:4, NIV).

Soon the group came to the Garden of Gethsemane, and here Jesus did something that was humanly unexpected. This is how Matthew recorded both his actions and statements: "Sit here while I go over there and pray." He then "took Peter and the two sons of Zebedee along with him, and he began to be sorrowful and troubled. Then he said to them 'My soul is overwhelmed with sorrow to the point of death. Stay here and keep watch with me.' Going a little farther, he fell with his face to the ground" (Matt. 26:36-38, NIV).

After revealing to Peter, James, and John the depths of the sorrow he felt, he left them, perhaps by a gnarled trunk of an olive tree, and went "a little farther"—Luke says "a stone's throw beyond them, knelt down and prayed" (22:41, NIV).

Beneath the shade of the olive tree where Jesus had left them, the three members of the inner circle listened as he, according to Matthew 26:39, prayed:

> My Father, if it is possible, may this cup be taken
> from me. Yet not as I will, but as you will (NIV).

No one, of course, knows the exact hour that Jesus first soiled his knees on the soil of Gethsemane at the beginning of this time of soul-searching. But it must have been about midnight. That means, according to our time, it was almost

April 7. This is because our days are from midnight to midnight; but in the Jewish system where a day was from sunset to sunset, it was still the fourteenth of Nisan.

How did the three fishermen respond? They went to sleep! Having finished his prayer, Jesus went over to the three. Finding them asleep, he addressed Peter: "Could you men not keep watch with me for one hour?" (Matt. 26:40, NIV).

Returning to his own private spot, Jesus prayed again. This time his prayer indicates that his own desires were gradually meshing with those of the Father. Listen! "My Father, if it is not possible for this cup to be taken away unless I drink it, may your will be done" (v. 42).

Rising from his knees, he returned to those whom he had asked to watch and pray with him. What did he find? They were sound asleep! This time, being an understanding person, and knowing that "their eyes were heavy" he did not awaken them.

After going back to his chosen place of prayer, Matthew reported that he "prayed the third time, saying the same thing" (v. 43).

Returning again to the three dead-to-the-world apostles-to-be, he was still kind: "Are you still sleeping and resting? Look, the hour is near, and the Son of Man is betrayed into the hands of sinners. Rise, let us go! Here comes my betrayer!" (v. 46).

Even though the three had failed him three times by not watching, he *still* needed them, and asked them to go with him. The time? Probably early Friday morning at perhaps 2 A.M.

As he shook the sleep out of his eyes, Simon Peter who, a few hours before, had boasted, "I am ready to go with you to prison and death," must have felt a sting of humiliation as he glanced at the tear-streaked cheeks of Jesus and realized that he had slept during one of his teacher's most excruciating hours. Did Peter realize that Jesus' quivering voice that sobbed "not my will but thine be done" indicated the first wrenching pains of the indescribable travail he was entering, a travail that would pay the price, and earn the redemption of his bride the church? Undoubtedly, he did not.

As Peter and the other fishermen stood transfixed with Jesus, Peter stared as Judas, now the incarnation of evil, approached. The scene was made even more horrible by the fact that the former treasurer of the Twelve was backed by a "large crowd armed with swords and clubs, sent from the chief priests and elders of the people" (Matt. 26:47, NIV).

While Peter gaped, Judas stretched out his arms; and, forcing a smile, said, "Greetings, Rabbi!" (v. 49, NIV). Then he embraced and kissed the man who had given him the piece of bread pressed into the shape of a spoon in the Upper Room.

What kind of thoughts were grinding in the mind of Peter at this time? Was he thinking about the way Jesus had washed his feet? We don't know. The probability is that he was reliving the two times Jesus had awakened him while he slept. On the first occasion, he had addressed him personally and then in a voice heavy with kindness had asked: "Could you not keep watch with me for one hour?" (Matt. 26:40, NIV).

Those words, sheathed with indescribable love and hurt. He must someway atone for his sin. But what could he do? Suddenly, his impulsive nature grabbed him. From his belt he snatched a sword from its scabbard. Then, aiming at the servant of the high priest, he swung with all the power his broad shoulders could deliver. But his strength was more effective than his aim, for he only managed to slash off the right ear of the servant of the high priest.

(Curiously, even though all the gospel writers mention that someone cut off the servant's ear, Doctor Luke is the only one who indicated that it was his "right" ear—and that Jesus healed it. (Luke 22:50-5). Moreover, John alone mentioned that it was Peter who swung the sword).

According to Matthew "all the disciples forsook him, and fled" (26:56). Two verses later, however, he wedged in: "But Peter followed him afar off." At this point John gives us a more detailed picture: "Simon Peter and another disciple were following Jesus. Because this disciple—[obviously

John]—was known to the high priest, he went with Jesus into the high priest's courtyard, but Peter had to wait outside at the door" (18:15-16, NIV).

Since it was nearly 4 A.M. and a little chilly, Simon Peter shuffled over to a fire to warm his hands. He had been clearly shaken by the events of the last few hours. On the outside he tried to appear calm; but on the inside he was almost paralyzed with fear. Suddenly, as he was toasting his hands and desperately trying not to look into the faces of the servants and officials who were also sitting or standing by the fire, a servant girl studied him closely. Their eyes met. "This man was with him," she announced (Luke 22:56).

"Woman, I don't know him" snapped Peter angrily.

The writers who described this drama did so with some apparent contradictions. We will quote all of them from the NIV. Matthew: "Now Peter was *sitting* out in the courtyard" (26:69). Mark: "While Peter was *below* in the courtyard" (14:66). Luke: "But when they had kindled a fire in the middle of the courtyard and had *sat* down together, Peter sat down with them" (22:55). John: "As Simon Peter *stood* warming himself, he was asked, 'You are not one of his disciples, are you?' " (18:25).

What is the solution to these apparent discrepancies by the gospel writers? All of them are right! Nervous Peter was *below* in the courtyard, as Mark reported. And he did *sit* down as both Matthew and Luke indicated. John was also correct when he wrote that his friend Peter "*stood* warming himself."

During the intensity of this life-or-death drama Peter twisted and turned, stood, bit his lip—and sat.

Since Peter and John alone among the eleven disciples had followed Jesus after he was arrested and taken to the palace of Caiaphas, let's see how John remembered the occasion when he wrote his Gospel. Again we will quote exclusively from the New International Version.

" 'You are not one of his disciples, are you?' the girl at the door asked Peter. He replied, 'I am not.'

"It was cold, and the servants and officials stood around a fire they had made to keep warm. Peter was also standing with them, warming himself" (18:17-18)

At this brink of the tightening drama, Luke adds a touch that intensifies it by informing us that as Peter warmed his hands, he also had a view of what was taking place in the hall of Caiaphas (22:60). Let us therefore borrow the eyes and ears of Peter and both view and listen to some of the things that must have, like the fires of hell, burned in his heart:

> Then they spit in his face and struck him with their fists. Others slapped him and said, Prophesy to us, Christ. Who hit you? (Matt. 26:67).

To this, Luke added another detail:

> They blindfolded him. . . . And the guards took him and beat him (22:64).

Luke's research included another fragment:

> They said many other insulting things to him (v. 65).

While this was going on, Peter was approached the second time. Matthew wrote: "Then he went out to the gateway, where another girl saw him and said to the people there, 'This fellow was with Jesus of Nazareth.'

"He denied it again with an oath: 'I don't *know* the man!' " (26:71-72)

After an hour had slowly, ever so slowly, grumbled by after he had entered the courtyard, Peter glanced across the city wall toward the east, and there, lighting the top of the Mount of Olives, he noticed the first crimson fingers of the morning sun.

His eyes had barely noticed those dim fragments of light when a man who was standing nearby—John identified him as "one of the high priest's servants, a relative of the man whose ear Peter had cut off—challenged him, 'Didn't I see you with him in the olive grove?' " (18:26). He "went up to

Peter and said, 'Surely you are one of them, for your accent [Mark and Luke add that he identified him as a Galilean] gives you away' " (Matt. 26:73).

Facing his third accuser, Peter's lips tightened and his knuckles turned white. Then he half-shouted as he "began to call curses on himself and he swore to them, 'I don't know the man!' " (v. 74).

At that moment, a rooster stretched its neck, lifted its head, and began to crow. Then Peter remembered the words of Jesus: "I tell you the truth . . . today—yes tonight—before the rooster crows twice you yourself will disown me three times" (Mark 14:30).

The wake-up bird of the barnyard had just crowed the second time when Peter glanced furtively toward the hall of Caiaphas. And at that moment "the Lord turned and looked straight at Peter. Then Peter remembered the word the Lord had spoken to him: 'Before the rooster crows today, you will disown me three times.' And he went outside and wept bitterly" (Luke 22:61-62).

Eyes blinded by tears, Peter stumbled through the gate. Memories of his actions during the last six or seven hours began to leer at him. They pointed accusing fingers and in mocking tones jeered: "And so you boasted 'Even if I have to die with you, I will never disown you' " (Mark 14:72, paraphrase) "Ho! Ho! Ho!

"Remember that first maid? She was a nice looking girl! And how about the second maid. She was also easy on the eyes. And how about that servant who was related to Malchus, the one whose ear you sliced off?

"Simon Peter, you're not a rock! You're not even an ooze of slime! In the last six hours you went to sleep three times while Jesus was pouring out his heart in Gethsemane and you denied that you even knew him three times. That means in the last six hours you've sinned at least double that number of times. In addition, you cursed. You are worse than the vilest murderer who ever lived. You ought to get a rope and hang yourself."

Can you answer?
1. On what days of the week did these scenes take place?
2. Did Jesus wash the disciples' feet *before* or *after* supper?
3. What valley did they cross as Jesus led the way to Gethsemane?
4. Why were the tombs on their way to Gethsemane whitewashed?
5. Which disciples entered Gethsemane? How far from them did Jesus kneel to pray?
6. How long was Peter in the courtyard of Caiaphas.
7. What kind of accent was Peter accused of having?

7

Peter's Bitter, Bitter Cup

Lingering outside the gate, Peter watched as Jesus was led northwestward toward the Praetorium. It was a little more than one-fourth of a mile away. As the mob with their prisoner passed him, he was horrified by the intense lines of joy that creased almost all their faces.

The leaders acted as if they had just captured the most notorious criminal in the world and were on their way to claim a reward. He was also unnerved at the painful way in which Jesus was bound. As he watched, a line from Isaiah may have seeped back into his mind:

"He was oppressed, and he was afflicted, yet he opened not his mouth: he is brought as a lamb to the slaughter" (53:7).

As Peter watched, a fresh flow of tears meandered down his cheeks and dripped on his gown. Unable to quench his tears, Peter followed the mob at a *safe* distance. While he shuffled along, memories from the Garden skidded into his mind.

He remembered that just after he, along with James and John had reached Gethsemane, Jesus had said to them: "My soul is overwhelmed with sorrow to the point of death. Stay here and keep watch with me" (Matt. 26:38, NIV). Now, as Peter's eyes followed the eager throng made up of members of the Sanhedrin along with get-on-the-bandwagon riffraff, those words sawed back and forth in his heart. The mental saw of memories of his sins during the previous seven hours kept rhythm with his steps: "I-denied-the-Lord-three-times. I-went-to-sleep-three-times. I-denied-the-Lord-three-times. I-went-to-sleep-three-times. I-I-stained-my-mouth-with-the-dreadful-oaths-of-my youth. I-denied-the Lord. I-I-I de-denied t-th-the L-o-r . . . L-o-r-d."

Peter tried desperately to forget those past hours. But he could not. Each memory was indelible, and more bitter than gall. Then another uninvited memory began to saw back and forth in his heart. It was devastating.

Just as he had been dozing off the first time, he had heard the anguished voice of Jesus. Quivering with pain, it sobbed: "My Father, if it is possible, may this cup be taken from me. Yet not as I will, but as you will" (v. 39).

Then he remembered that Jesus had awakened them. "Could you men not keep watch with me for one hour?" he had asked him. (v. 40). Jesus had then generously found an excuse for them: "The spirit is willing, but the body is weak" (v. 41).

Recollections of the mildness of that rebuke slashed and sawed even deeper into his heart.

Ah, but then he had gone to sleep a second time. This time just before losing consciousness, Jesus' voice tumbled into his mind: in this second moment of agony, Jesus' prayer was slightly different than his first prayer:

"My Father, if it is not possible for this cup to be taken from me unless I drink it, *may your will be done*" (v. 42).

Peter tried desperately to exclude these memories from his mind; but he could not. They continued to saw in his brain as he strode along: "While-Jesus-prayed-you-slept. While-Jesus-prayed-you slept. Then-you-denied-him-three-times. You-denied-him. You-denied-him. He-healed-your-mother-in-law. But-you denied-him. He-paid-your-taxes. But-you-denied-him. You-denied-him. You-denied . . ."

Suddenly the mob was at the Praetorium; and as Peter stood on tiptoe, he saw the Roman Governor Pontius Pilate face the mob. Peter was so far away he couldn't hear what the man in the toga was saying. But presently the mob left the Praetorium and headed south to the nearby palace of Herod Antipas. (Antipas was a son of Herod the Great, the one who strangled his own sons because they, through their mother Mariamne, had royal blood and he did not (See Ludwig 1983).

A little braver now, Peter elbowed his way nearly to the front. There, for the first time in his life, he saw Herod Antipas. Dressed in all his regalia, King Herod smiled broadly as he looked down on Jesus. Anxiously, Peter listened to every word that was said. Luke described the scene in the twenty-third chapter of his gospel: "When Herod saw Jesus, he was greatly pleased, because for a long time he had been wanting to see him. From what he had heard about him, he hoped to see him perform a miracle. He plied him with many questions, but Jesus gave him no answer. The chief priests and the teachers of the law were standing there, vehemently accusing him" (v. 8-10, NIV).

As Peter watched and listened, he undoubtedly hoped that Jesus *would* perform a miracle. But the one who had calmed the sea, fed multitudes with a few loaves and fishes, and cleansed lepers remained silent.

Again, the Big Fisherman, remembered the words of Isaiah: "He was oppressed, and he was afflicted, yet he opened not his mouth" (53:7). As he looked at Jesus, Peter must have again wondered: *Could it be that this Jesus whom I have followed for the last three years is the fulfillment of that prophecy?*

But Peter didn't have much time to consider such thoughts; for, as he stood, transfixed, the soldiers dressed Jesus like a king. Then, as he stood, with an "elegant robe" flowing from his shoulders, they mocked him and sent him back to Pilate.

Peter returned to the Praetorium. This time Pilate, still on the fence and frightened, vainly sought a way to remain on the fence. Moreover, his anxiety had been increased by a note from his wife. The words on the wax tablet that a servant handed him were precise and to the point: "Don't have anything to do with this innocent man, for I have suffered a great deal today in a dream because of him" (Matt. 27:19, NIV).

Glassy-eyed, Pilate nervously made an inventory of his brain as he searched for a way to slip from the horns of this dilemma that had snagged him. Finally Peter noted the trace of a smile on his lips. Vainly trying to subdue the quiver in his voice, Pilate pointed out to the crowd that it was customary to release a condemned man on the occasion of the Passover.

The procurator whispered to an aide: "Go to the dungeon and bring him up. He's vicious. Make certain that he's chained."

As Peter watched, Barabbas—tradition declares that his first name was Jesus—was brought up. "Which of the two do you want me to release" (v. 21) asked the closely cropped Roman. He spoke hopefully. His proposition was clear. They could vote for the release of either Jesus Barabbas, the broken-nailed murderer, or Jesus Christ, the one who had fed the multitude, healed the sick, and in whom there was no guile.

The answer was immediate and tumultuous. Peter felt a wave of revulsion sweep over him as the masses, like a Greek chorus at the end of an act, shouted: "Barabbas! Barabbas! Barabbas! Give us Barabbas!"

"What shall I do, then, with Jesus who is called the Christ?" (v. 22) demanded Pilate.

"They all answered, 'Crucify him!' " (v. 22).

" 'Why? What crime has he committed?' " asked Pilate (v. 23).

"But they shouted all the louder, 'Crucify him!' " (v. 23).

Amidst the shouting of Crucify him! Crucify him! Pilate's skillful mind came up with a new idea. He sentenced Jesus to be flogged. Again Simon Peter shuffled over to a place near the post where this half-way death would be carried out. And once again memory hammered his brain to the rhythm of his steps: "I-went-to-sleep-three-times. I-denied-him-three-times. I-went-to-sleep-three-times. I-denied-him-three-times. I-cursed! I-cursed! I-cursed!"

The rhythms of those hammer-beats on his brain were like the clocks of doom.

All but blinded by tears, Peter watched as Jesus was chained to the post. Then he watched the heavy-chested Syrians pick up their whips. Not limited to thirty-nine stripes as Jewish law insisted, their only requirement was that they not kill him.

Blinded by tears as the whips swished and scooped paths of flesh, Peter felt sick at the stomach. As the swishing and scooping continued, he remembered that Jesus had said to him in the Garden: "My soul is overwhelmed with sorrow to the point of death. Stay here and keep watch with me." But instead of watching, he had gone to sleep. Then he had been awakened by Jesus, but he had gone to sleep again. Then he had made the crowd angrier than ever by hacking off a man's ear. Then he had denied him three times.

As the swishing, and scooping, and gouging, and swishing, and scooping, and gouging continued, Jesus' back became a wide bloody mass. In addition, his body slipped lower and lower on the post.

Finally, the officer in command said: "That's enough. If we kill him the mob won't have the opportunity of jeering at him on the cross."

After they had removed him from the post, they led him back to Pilate. As Peter stumbled along at a safe distance from Jesus, another passage of Isaiah filtered into his mind: "But he was wounded for our transgressions, he was bruised for our iniquities: the chastisement of our peace was upon him; *and with his stripes we are healed*" (53:5).

As he viewed Jesus' wounds from a distance, Peter was tormented by one thought: *Is this the one Isaiah had in mind when he wrote his prophecy?* It seems strange that Peter would be subject to such doubts when we remember that at Caesarea Philippi he had boldly said: "You are the Christ, the Son of the living God" (Matt. 16:16, NIV).

That he was the Son of God is abundantly clear. Nevertheless, even the finest and most dedicated Christians are tormented from time to time with honest doubts.

Back at the Praetorium, Peter watched Pilate as he filled a basin with water, and ceremoniously washed his hands. Then he heard him say: "I am innocent of this man's blood. . . . It is your responsibility!" (27:24, NIV).

Utterly delighted with this decision, "All the people answered, 'Let his blood be on us and on our children!' " (v. 25).

"Then the governor's soldiers took Jesus into the Praetorium and gathered the whole company of soldiers around him. They stripped him and put a scarlet robe on him, and then twisted together a crown of thorns and set it on his head. They put a staff in his right hand and knelt in front of him and mocked him, 'Hail, king of the Jews,' they said. They spit on him, and took the staff and struck him on the head again and again. After they had mocked him, they took off the robe and put his own clothes on him. Then they led him away to crucify him" (vv. 27-31).

Half blinded by tears, Peter followed Jesus as he, with the cross—actually it was the *patibulum* (the cross piece that would be fastened to the *stripes*—the upright that remained permanently in the ground) across his shoulder, staggered over the *Via Dolorosa* (the Way of Suffering; see Ludwig 1989, 51-60 for a discussion of the construction of the cross and of the crucifixion).

(Today, this route has fourteen stations. Each station represents a certain event that took place as Jesus was led to Calvary. Since there is divided opinion about the spot where Jesus was crucified, the entire Via Dolorosa is not accepted by all believers. The current fourteen stations were not established until the nineteenth century.)

Jesus had not gone far until he began to sway beneath the weight of the patibulum. (Its estimated weight is approximately 60 pounds). As Jesus careened from side to side, Simon Peter unconsciously did the same. In a mysterious way it seemed that he was walking in tandem with Jesus.

All at once Jesus stumbled and fell. Peter shuddered. Then a wild idea scrambled into his mind. *Perhaps he should elbow forward and carry the patibulum for him.* But no, this was an impossibility. His spirit was willing. His flesh was weak. As a lad, he had seen a row of men hanging on crosses. He could never forget their spine-tingling screams. For years memories of their shrieks had clothed themselves into dreams that had awakened him during the night.

The fully armed centurion was caught off guard. If he asked a Jew to pick up the patibulum, the man would be defiled, and thus would be unable to partake of the Passover Feast. What was he to do? At that moment, he saw Simon of Cyrene, a city in North Africa. Pointing at him with his sword, he said, "Hey, you, pick up that cross piece. Help him!"

As Peter watched him stoop down and pick up the patibulum, his heart began to thump. The muscle-laced black man (strong legend insists that he was black), picked up the heavy cyprus plank, placed it on his shoulder, and with an arm around Jesus' waist headed toward the hill shaped like a skull.

In the name of truth and mercy, why didn't he, Peter, help Jesus? The answer was clear. He wasn't helping Jesus because he was a coward! In his time of need, Jesus had paid his taxes. In his time of need Jesus had healed his mother-in-law. In his time of need after he had fished all night without catching a single fish, Jesus told him "Put out into deep water, and let down the nets for a catch" (Luke 5:4, NIV). After he obeyed, he snared so many fish the net began to break. Indeed, there were so many fish his boat almost sank, and he had to summon another boat that also began to sink. That day, his eyes danced with joy as he counted the money he had earned. But now that Jesus was in desperate need, he had not offered help.

Continuing to remain at a safe distance, Peter shuffled forward toward a gate that led outside the wall. Again, as he kept up with the mob, the hated litany came back and kept harmony with his feet: "While-he-agonized-I-slept. While-he-agonized-I-slept. I-denied-him-three-times. I-denied-him-three-times. I-denied-him-three-times. I-cursed-I-cursed-I-cursed."

The mob stopped at the top of a hill shaped like a skull. As Peter stood on tiptoe, he noticed that John and Mary, the mother of Jesus, were standing only a few yards away where Jesus was lying on the ground.

All at once Peter heard the thump of a hammer as spikes were hammered through Jesus' wrists (See Ludwig 1989, 65). As he listened to those dreadful thumps, he noticed that Mary shuddered after each one. He also noticed that John was comforting her.

As Jesus—his arms stretched out on the patibulum—was lifted and the patibulum was secured in the stipes, it was according to Mark about "the third hour" (15:25). That is, it was about 9 A.M. according to our reckoning.

Still remaining *afar off*, Peter watched, suffered—and wept. As the slow as eternity hours ever so slowly meandered by, Peter continued to watch and listen. In the midst of his agony Jesus began to speak. Peter was too far away to hear everything he said, but his words: *"Father, forgive them; for they know not what they do"* (Luke 23:34) reached him, loud and clear.

Those words stabbed deep into his heart, for the antecedent of Jesus' pronoun *them* included Judas who betrayed him; the false witnesses who testified against him; Caiaphas who led the mob; the soldiers who beat him and mocked him and drove the spikes through his hands and feet; the gamblers who were gambling at the foot of the stipes; the thieves who mocked him; the mob that was jeering him. But, alas, that word *them* didn't include him!

Why? Because he was *not* innocent through ignorance! Once again his confession at Caesarea Philippi came back to him. It wrapped around him in the manner of a python. As his eyes flooded and his nose dripped, he remembered them syllable by syllable: "Thou—art—the—Christ,—the—Son—of—the—living—God" (Matt. 16:18).

Yes, he, Simon Peter, knew that Jesus was "the only begotten Son of God." This meant he was worse than Judas! This was so, for on the occasion of his confession at Caesarea Philippi, Judas, together with the other ten, had not understood that Jesus was indeed the Son of God.

Peter was thankful for the intense darkness that had covered the land, for it hid his swollen eyes and the deep lines in his face that were being formed by the conflict that was raging in his heart.

Wiping his eyes and blowing his nose again and again, Peter kept asking himself the same question: *What, oh what am I to do?*

As the battle raged his attention was suddenly captivated by the fact that even though it was dark, he saw Jesus lift his head and heard him cry in a loud voice "Eloi, Eloi, lama sabachthani?" (27:46, NIV). Peter was stunned, for he understood that those words in Hebrew meant: "My God, my God, why have you forsaken me" (Matt. 27:46, NIV).

Moments later, he heard Jesus' final piercing wail: "It is finished" (John 19:30), and saw his head slump forward.

Realizing that Jesus was dead, Peter disappeared. Where he went, no one knows. But we must conclude that wherever he went it was impossible for him to rid himself of the overflowing cup of bitter, bitter memories that continued to haunt his heart and brain.

Can you answer?
1. Who was the Roman Governor at this time?
2. Before which Herod did Jesus appeared? Who was his father?
3. What did Jesus say to Herod?
4. Name three ways in which Pilate tried to escape making a decision to crucify Jesus.
5. Who was Barabbas? What, according to legend was his first name?
6. Who ordered Jesus to be flogged?
7. What was the difference between the patibulum and the stipes?

8

Even So They Went Fishing!

Broad shoulders slumped, Simon Peter staggered away from the three crosses that were casting lengthening shadows from the summit of the hill with the hollow eyes of a skull. Bowed with guilt, Peter didn't quite know what to do.

As he zigzagged toward the city, he realized that when the sun touched the horizon it would be the fifteenth of Nisan, the beginning of the Passover Feast. Unlike Simon of Cyrene, he had not touched an instrument of death and thus was fully qualified to partake of the unleavened bread and the bitter herbs and the lamb that would be roasted in many homes.

Perhaps, he reasoned to himself, I will feel better when I get back with my fishermen friends. *Oh but what would he say to John who had lingered at the base of the cross and who, even though he was personally known by the high priest, had boldly comforted Jesus' mother Mary?*

John, too, had gone to sleep three times in the Garden. Even so, John had not cursed or denied Jesus!

What, oh what was he to do?

As he pondered what action to take, the faces of the ones who had heard his denials and oaths came to a focus in his mind. Again the memory of the dreadful crowing of the rooster dominated his thinking as did the memory of Jesus' admonition: "Simon, Simon, Satan has asked to sift you as wheat. But I have prayed for you, Simon, that your faith may not fail. . . . I tell you, Peter, before the rooster crows today you will deny three times that you know me" (Luke 22:31, 33, NIV).

Head bowed in shame, Peter continued on to his Passover lodgings. He'd just stretched out on his bed when he heard the three blasts of the ram's horn and knew that the Passover Sabbath had come and that it was now the fifteenth of Nisan. As he relaxed, the time that Jesus' eyes met his eyes while he was in the courtyard and Jesus was in the Palace of Caiaphas came back to him.

He had known Jesus for three years. He had seen his eyes fill with pain and with laughter and with authority; but never had he seen them overflowing with compassion and understanding as they had on that occasion. In his heart, Peter knew that he would never forget that look of compassion; and, yes, that look of utter and complete forgiveness.

But did Jesus have the power to forgive sins? That question haunted him.

As Peter turned it over in his mind he remembered an occasion when Jesus was preaching in Capernaum. He had been amazed at his neighbors and friends who had crowded into the house where his Lord and Master was preaching. In the midst of one of his discourses "Some men came, bringing to him a paralytic, carried by four of them" (Mark 2:3, NIV). Since there was no room for the crippled man in the house, his friends "made an opening in the roof above Jesus and, after digging through it, lowered the mat the paralyzed man was lying on" (v. 4).

Jesus was so overwhelmed by the man's faith, he exclaimed, "Son, your sins are forgiven" (v. 5).

All of this angered the teachers of the law who were sitting nearby. Knowing what these men of learning were thinking, Jesus said: "Which is easier: to say to the paralytic, 'Your sins are forgiven,' or to say, 'Get up, take your mat and walk?' *But that you may know that the Son of man has authority on earth to forgive sins.* . . .' He said to the paralytic, 'I tell you, get up, take your mat and go home.'

"[The paralytic] got up, took his mat and walked out in full view of them all. This amazed everyone and they praised God saying, 'We have never seen anything like this!' " (vv. 9-12).

Considering all of this, Peter was downcast by the idea that it is as hard to forgive sins as it is to heal a paralytic. That *was* a discouraging thought. If this was the case, he could *never* be forgiven, for he had gone to sleep three times, and he had denied that he even knew Jesus three times. Moreover, he had forsaken Jesus as he died in agony on the cross.

But as Peter pondered, another fact must have slammed into his mind. The fact was that while the learned teachers' jaws sagged, the paralyzed man had stood up, and with his mat in his arms had walked out of the house.

Did this mean that if Jesus could heal a paralytic, he could also forgive sins? Undoubtedly it did! Even so, didn't animal sacrifices have to be made in order to atone for sin? And on the Day of Atonement didn't a scapegoat have to be loaded with the sins of Israel and then be driven into the wilderness in order that it, along with its burden of sin, would be lost? Yes, this was true, and he had known these facts all his life.

How, then, could Jesus forgive sins without making animal sacrifices or sending a scapegoat into the wilderness? (See Ludwig 1989, 79-83).

The problem was a mysterious conundrum. He rolled and tossed as he tried to solve it. Then early in the morning after a rooster had crowed, an early memory that had laid dormant in an obscure corner of his brain suddenly bloomed into life.

Religious from the time they were boys, both Peter and his brother Andrew had been followers of John the Baptist. One day when this man who wore camel's hair and subsisted on locusts and wild honey saw Jesus coming toward him, he said, "Look, the *Lamb of God*, who takes away the sin of the world" (John 1:29, NIV).

That was, indeed, a startling statement; for John's followers were all familiar with the way Isaiah had referred to the coming Messiah as "a lamb [led] to the slaughter" (53:7, NIV).

John the Baptist was so convinced that Jesus was the "Lamb of God" that he gave this testimony:

> I saw the Spirit come down from heaven as a dove and remain on him. I would not have known him, except that the one who sent me to baptize with water told me, 'The man on whom you see the Spirit come down and remain is he who will baptize you with the Holy Spirit.' *I have seen and testify that this is the Son of God"* (John 1:32-34, NIV).

These thoughts comforted Peter, but he was still not solidly convinced. On the fifteenth of Nisan, Peter, like the others attended the Passover Feast. In the back of his mind, he remembered that Jesus had promised that he would arise from the dead on the third day. But the evidence indicates that he was not overly concerned in this matter. Perhaps, he may have reasoned that Jesus' statements about his resurrection were to be merely taken in a spiritual, rather than in a literal way. After viewing the temple Jesus had said: "Destroy this temple, and I will raise it again in three days" (2:19). Stunned, the Jews exclaimed: 'It has taken forty-six years to build this temple, and you are going to raise it in three days?' " (2:20).

Angered, his critics made mental notes of what he had said.

The disciples, however, accustomed to Jesus' manner of speech, realized that "the temple he had spoken of was his body" (v. 21).

Early on Sunday morning while Peter and John were together, they heard a loud thump at the door. Facing a panting Mary Magdalene, they were both shocked to hear her stammer: "T-they h-have taken away t-the Lord out of the sepulchre, and we know not where they have l-l-laid h-him" (20:2).

John and Peter then took off for the tomb. How did they know where it was? Because they both knew as John recorded in, his gospel, "Now in the place where he was crucified there was a garden; and in the garden a new sepulchre, wherein was never man yet laid" (19:41-42).

As they ran, John outran Peter. Why? An interesting conjecture is that as they ran, a trio of wake-up roosters began to crow; and their crowing reminded Peter of his three denials.

That hideous memory might have slowed him down for a pace or two. But even though John reached the tomb first, this Son of Thunder allowed Peter to precede him inside.

Yes, the tomb was empty just as Mary Magdalene had said.

To whom did the resurrected Christ appear first? To Mary Magdalene! (Mark 16:10). As I pointed out in *At the Tomb*, (p. 99), Jesus did not appear first to Peter as one might assume by a hurried reading of Luke 24:33-34, or 1 Corinthians 15:5. Both these writers merely said that he was seen by Cephas. Nonetheless, he was seen more often by Cephas than anyone else! Let's reread the passages that indicate that this is true. I have put in italics the places where Peter's presence is indicated:

> He appeared to *Peter* and then to the *Twelve*. (1 Cor. 15:15, NIV).

> Later Jesus appeared to the *Eleven* as they were eating (Mark 16:14, NIV).

> "[Those who were on their way to Emmaus] got up and returned at once to Jerusalem. There they found the *Eleven* and those with them assembled together.... While they were still talking ... Jesus stood among them and said to them 'Peace be with you' " (Luke 24:33-36, NIV).

> Now Thomas (called Didymus), one of the *Twelve* was not with the disciples when Jesus came. So the other disciples told him, "We have seen the

Lord!" He said to them, "Unless I see the nail marks in his hands and put my finger where the nails were, and put my hand into his side, I will not believe it" (John 20:24-25, NIV).

A week later the *disciples* were in the house again, and Thomas was with them. Though the doors were locked, Jesus came and stood among them and said, "Peace be with you!" Then he said to Thomas, "Put your finger here; see my hands. Reach out your hand and put it in my side. Stop doubting and believe" (John 20:26-27, NIV).

During that entire week of Passover celebrations, Peter had seen the resurrected Christ again and again. And not only had he seen him, but he had eaten with him. Moreover, he had seen him appear in a room even though the doors were closed. The memory of the time he had shown his wounds to Thomas and asked him to examine them was very real; and he knew that he could never forget the look of ecstasy that had covered the Twin's face when he cried out: "My Lord and my God!" (v. 28).

But what did Peter do with this knowledge? As far as we know, he didn't do anything. True, he, along with the other disciples had approached Thomas because he had been absent when Jesus appeared to them in spite of locked doors, and assured him, "we have seen the Lord!" (v. 25).

There is no record, however, that Peter at this time, mentioned to anyone else that he had seen the resurrected Christ. Why? Other than for the fact that the disciples feared the Jews, there seems to be no apparent reason for his and their silence. The week of Passover was certainly an excellent time to evangelize. The city of Jerusalem throbbed with pilgrims from all over the world.

It would seem that somewhere in the crowded temple or on the streets Peter could have motioned to an acquaintance to follow him into a secret place and there at least whispered to him the good news.

The good news about his visits with the Resurrected Christ would have brought a sparkle into many eyes, especially of those whom Jesus had healed. But instead of relaying this good news as one would relay the good news if his dying wife had been healed, Simon Peter, the Rock, had said: "I go a-fishing" (21:3).

His suggestion pleased those who were with him. Years later when John wrote the Fourth Gospel he felt inspired to include their names. The group included Thomas, Nathaniel, James and John, and "two other of his disciples" (v. 2). This means that there were seven of them.

As we view them climbing into a boat in order to fish in the lake—for some unknown reason on this occasion John called lake Galilee "the sea of Tiberias"—we wonder why all of them were not out telling their friends about the many appearances of Jesus. Being in Galilee, they were comparatively safe from their enemies in Jerusalem, several day's journey to the south.

In that most of them were experienced at fishing, it is reasonable to surmise that they had the right kind of nets and knew exactly where to go during this season of the year.

But the only things their work had gained them were an empty boat and aching backs and shoulders. They looked at one another and shrugged. Then the scene changed:

"Morning came, and there stood Jesus on the beach, but the disciples did not know that it was Jesus. He called out to them, 'Friends have you caught anything?' They answered 'No.' He said, 'Shoot the net to starboard, and you will make a catch.' They did so, and found they could not haul the net, there were so many fish in it. Then the disciple whom Jesus loved said to Peter, 'It is the Lord!' When Simon Peter heard that, he wrapped his coat about him (for he had stripped) and plunged into the sea. The rest of them came on in the boat, towing the net full of fish; for they were not far from the land, only about a hundred yards" (21:4-8, NEB).

Upon reaching shore they found a charcoal fire burning with fish laid on it. (At this point, F. F. Bruce has suggested that perhaps the Greek word for fish *opsarian*, might, just might be in the singular). Great expositor that he was, he had a reason for this suggestion that we shall see.

Returning to the NEB we read: "Jesus said, 'Bring some of your catch.' Simon Peter went aboard and dragged the net to land, full of big fish, a hundred and fifty-three of them; and yet, many as they were, the net was not torn" (v. 10).

At this point, Peter must have wondered why Jesus asked that they move their catch. Could it not have remained on the edge of the shore where it was? True, the one fish Jesus had prepared might have been insufficient for eight hungry men. Nevertheless, if Jesus had caught and prepared a single fish on his own, why could he not have caught and prepared another?

Was Jesus doing something that they would only fully understand later? It is possible that Peter remembered that when Jesus washed his feet in the Upper Room he had remarked: "You do not realize what I am doing, but later you will understand" (John 13:7, NIV).

Also, on a previous occasion, when Jesus in his resurrected body had visited the ten disciples, he asked them, " 'Have you anything here to eat?' They offered him a piece of fish they had cooked, which he took and ate before their eyes" (Luke 24:42, NEB).[1]

Did any of the ten—the passage says eleven but Thomas was missing—wonder why he asked them for something to eat when they knew that he was quite capable of providing something to eat by himself?[2] No one knows; but the fact that he asked *them* for food just as he had asked them to move their catch is quite significant.

Following their meal, Jesus' oft-quoted conversation with Peter took place. (F. F. Bruce commented that after Jesus and the disciples had eaten, Jesus took Peter for a short walk. His conversation with him was thus an isolated one.) This is how the NEB records their exchange of words:

> After breakfast, Jesus said to Simon Peter, "Simon, son of John, do you love me more than all else?" "Yes, Lord," he answered, "you know

that I love you." "Then *feed* my *lambs*," he said. A second time he asked, "Simon son of John, do you love me?" "Yes, Lord, you know that I love you." "Then *tend* my *sheep*." A third time he said, "Simon son of John, do you love me?" Peter was hurt that he asked him a third time, "Do you love me?" "Lord," he said, "you know everything; you know I love you." Jesus said, *"Feed* my *sheep"* (John 21:15-17, NEB).

F. F. Bruce has contributed a tongue-in-cheek comment about the essence of the above: "When [Peter was] called from his occupation of catching fish to be a follower of Jesus, he was told that thenceforth he would catch men (Luke 5:10; c.f. Mark 1:17). Now to the evangelist's hook there is added the pastor's crook, so that as often has been said, Peter proceeded to fulfill his double commission 'by hook and crook' " (405).

After Jesus had disappeared, did Peter immediately start to use his fisherman's hook or his shepherd's crook to evangelize?

If he did, there is no such evidence in Scripture. Why? That question will be answered in the next chapter!

Can you answer?
1. Why would Peter wonder if Jesus had the power to forgive sin?
2. How did Jesus indicate that it is as hard to forgive as it is to heal a paralyzed person?
3. Who said, "Behold the Lamb of God?"
4. On what day of the month did the Passover begin?
5. As Peter and John ran to the tomb, who reached there first?
6. What kind of a fire did Jesus use to broil the fish?
7. What do we mean when we say that Jesus told Peter to use both a hook and a crook when he evangelized and fed the sheep?

9

They Waited, and Waited, and Waited

Together with the five hundred, Peter was addressed again by the resurrected Christ. This episode, mentioned only by Paul (1 Cor. 15:6), took place on a mountain in Galilee. Here Jesus uttered his explicit command:

> All authority in heaven and on earth has been given to me. Therefore go and make disciples of all nations, baptizing them in the name of the Father and of the Son and of the Holy Spirit, and teaching them to obey everything I have commanded you. And surely I will be with you always, to the very end of the age. (Matt. 28:18-20, NIV).

This, however, was not the last time the eleven disciples were with the resurrected Christ. In Acts 1:4-5, Luke reported: "On one occasion, while he was eating with them, he gave them this command: 'Do not leave Jerusalem, but *wait* for the gift my Father promised, which you have heard me speak about. For John baptized with water, but in a few days you will be baptized with the Holy Spirit' " (v. 5). Then, forty days after Easter Sunday, while the disciples were on the Mount of Olives, Jesus made a sudden appearance. As they watched, Jesus defied gravity and "was taken up before their very eyes, and a cloud hid him from their sight" (1:9).

(This occasion, celebrated by Anglican, Roman Catholic, and Eastern churches as Ascension Day, is observed each year on Thursday, forty days after Easter).

Dismayed, the apostles-to-be were transfixed as they stared upward at the cloud in which Jesus had disappeared. Luke wrote: "They were looking intently up into the sky as he was going, when suddenly two men dressed in white stood beside them. 'Men of Galilee,' they said, 'why do you stand here looking into the sky? This same Jesus, who has been taken from you into heaven, will come back in the same way you have seen him go into heaven' " (Acts 1:10-11, NIV).

The disciples then returned to Jerusalem and "they went up into an upper room, where abode both Peter, and James, and John, and Andrew, Philip, and Thomas, Bartholomew, and Matthew, James the son of Alphaeus, and Simon Zelotes, and Judas the brother of James" (1:13, KJV).

But where was this upper room? It is generally assumed that it was *the* Upper Room where Jesus celebrated the Last Supper with the Twelve. Is this correct? Campbell Morgan in his book *The Acts of the Apostles* does not agree. Let's read and compare the passages he has suggested on page 24 to prove his point:

> And they worshiped him, and returned to Jerusalem with great joy: and were *continually* in the *temple*, praising and blessing God (Luke 24:52-53).
>
> And when the *day* of *Pentecost* was fully come, they were all with one accord in *one place* (Acts 2:1). (The obvious place for a Jew to be on that day was in the temple!)
>
> And they, continuing daily with one accord in the *temple*, and breaking bread from house to house, did eat their meat with gladness and singleness of heart (Acts 2:46).

Since it is arguable that they waited in the temple rather than in the Upper Room, the next questions is Who was there? Although Luke named the eleven disciples plus a few others: "Mary the mother of Jesus . . . and . . . [Jesus'] brethren," he merely estimated that there were "*about* one hundred and twenty" (Acts 2:14:15).

The number one hundred twenty seems large in comparison to the Twelve. But remembering that Jesus had appeared to "above five hundred brethren at once" the number is insignificant. It is less that one fourth of them! As we try to name the one hundred or so Luke did not mention, our imaginations slip into high gear.

It would seem logical to believe that both Nicodemus and Joseph of Arimathea were there as well as the other two Marys who lingered at Calvary with Mary the mother of Jesus. And how about Simon of Cyrene who helped carry his cross as well as the widow who dropped two mites in the treasury and the paralyzed man who was let down through the roof in the house at Capernaum?

No one can be dogmatic about the answer to these questions. All we can be sure *about* is that there were about one hundred and twenty present.

One of the numerous miracles of this occasion is that the one hundred and twenty were allowed by the authorities and masses who had shouted "Crucify him! Crucify him!" to remain in one central place—particularly a public place—unmolested. This is especially apparent when we realize that just a short time before when Jesus appeared to them and asked Thomas to examine his wounds, the "doors were locked" (John 20:26, NIV).

Another miracle is that Peter, without a single objection being made, was allowed to take a place of leadership among them. Doctor Luke briefly sketched what happened:

"It was during this time that Peter stood up before the assembled brotherhood, about one hundred and twenty in all, and said: 'My friends, the prophecy of Scripture was bound to come true, which the Holy Spirit, through the mouth of David, uttered about Judas who acted as guide to those who arrested Jesus. For he was one of our number and had his place in this ministry'" (Acts 1:15-17, NEB).

Peter then went on to tell how Judas had committed suicide and led the eleven disciples into a selection of one to take his place. The final choice was between Barsabbas and Matthias; and, as every Bible student knows, Matthias was elected.

But this election is not our concern right now. Instead, our concern centers on how it was possible for Peter to stand in the midst of the one hundred twenty and assume the responsibility of electing a candidate to take the place of Judas.

Consider some of the problems that must have chewed in his heart:

>1. From the temple area the Garden of Gethsemane was clearly evident. Did his mind go back to the way he had gone to sleep three times and hacked off a man's ear?

>2. As he spoke with the eyes of John, the Son of Thunder on him, did he wonder what John was thinking as he silently recalled his three denials?

>3. And what about Mary the mother of Jesus? Did he not feel uncomfortable as he saw her sitting there and realized that she knew that he had feared to approach the cross as her son was suffering the agonies of hell?

The truth is that the Holy Spirit was already in charge of the situation. From a *human* point of view, ever-loyal John, the one who had lingered with Mary at the foot of the cross and to whom Jesus had entrusted the care of his mother, should have been *the* leader and spokesperson. Most of us would have voted for John!

The Holy Spirit, however, decided otherwise. Campbell Morgan pointed out a subtle fact that tends to indicate this. Throughout the New Testament we generally read: Peter, James, and John. But on this occasion, as the eleven disciples were gathered to wait, Luke arranged their names in a different sequence: "Those present were Peter, John, James and Andrew" (Acts 1:13, NIV) (Campbell 18).

An even stronger indication that the Holy Spirit was already with them is given in the comment of Jesus after Peter's confession in Matthew 16:17. Said Jesus: "Blessed are you, Simon son of Jonah, for this was not revealed to you by man, *but by my Father in heaven*" (Matt. 16:17, NIV).

Another manifestation of the power of the Holy Spirit with the eleven prior to Pentecost is, as we pointed out in the beginning of this chapter, that the 120 were led to gather in one central and vital place without being molested.

As the 120 waited and waited and waited, we wonder what they might have been doing to pass the time. True, as Luke said, they "all continued with one accord in prayer and supplication" (Acts 1:14). Even so, there must have been intervals between meals and day-to-day errands.

Could it be that in one of those intervals the Twelve—Matthias had now taken the place of Judas—discussed the events when Jesus prepared their breakfast on the shore of the lake? We can easily imagine that one of them might have asked, "Why do you suppose the net didn't break when we pulled in those 153 enormous fish? I was there the other time when he told us 'put out into deep water and let down your nets for a catch' and when we did so we made 'a big haul of fish; and [our] nets began to split' " (Luke 5:4-6, NEB).

"Perhaps," another fisherman might have suggested, "he was telling us that when we became fishers for persons our nets would never break."

It is logical also to believe that as they waited they studied the Septuagint. We get hints of this both from Matthew and Peter. In his speech in which Peter related the story of Judas, he quoted from Psalm 69:25—"May their place be deserted; let there be no one to dwell in their tents" (NIV). Also from Psalm 109:8—"May his days be few; may another take his place of leadership."

In the gospel according to Matthew we constantly come

across such references to the Old Testament as: "Behold a virgin shall be with child" (1:23) from Isaiah 7:14—"Behold a virgin shall conceive, and bear a son, and shall call his name Immanuel."

Jesus' being born in Bethlehem (Matt. 2:1) was foretold in Micah 5:2—"But thou, Bethlehem Ephratah, though thou be little among the thousands of Judah, yet out of thee shall he come forth unto me that is to be ruler in Israel; whose goings forth have been from of old, from everlasting."

In the temple, numerous items and places reminded the 120 of the ministry of Jesus. They remembered the place where he threw the money changers out; the treasury where the widow cast in her two mites; the place near the temple where he had hidden when his enemies sought to stone him (John 8:59 and 12:36); and especially the torn veil that was suspended on hooks between the holy place and the holy of holies.

Since that enormous veil had been torn from the "top to the bottom" (Mark 15:38) at the moment of Jesus' death (v. 37), the place where it had hung was undoubtedly one of intense interest. This is because the veil screened the holy of holies, Israel's most sacred place, from the eyes of the masses. One can almost hear the questions that may have been asked by eager viewers as they stood with bowed heads before the remnants of the multi-colored curtain that had woven into it the winged features of the cherubim.

While wringing his hands, one can almost hear one of the group asking, "How can the high priest go before the Lord and pour the blood filled with the sins of Israel on the scapegoat that will be lost in the wilderness?"

"And w-what will I-I d-d-do with m-my s-s-s-sins if the D-day of A-tonement is no m-more?" wails another.

"And who" begs still another, "w-will be our go-between if the high priest cannot g-go into the secret holy of holies?"

If the future author of the Book of Hebrews had been there, is it not possible that as he pointed at the remnants of the curtain with a firm finger he might have said what he was later to write:

[Christ] did not enter by means of the blood of goats and calves; but he entered the *Most Holy Place once for all by his own blood having obtained eternal redemption.*

The blood of goats and bulls and the ashes of a heifer sprinkled on those who are ceremonially unclean sanctify them so that they are outwardly clean.

How much more, then, will the *blood of Christ, who through the eternal Spirit offered himself unblemished to God cleanse our consciences from acts that lead to death, so that we may serve the living God!*

For this reason Christ is the mediator of a *new covenant*, that those who are called may receive the promised eternal inheritance—*now that he has died as a ransom to set them free from the sins committed under the first covenant* (Hebrews 9:12-15, NIV). (See Ludwig 1989, p. 7 for a more detailed account of the Day of Atonement).

Others were worried about the time. We can imagine an old man asking, "Did Jesus say how long we should wait?" And another adding: "The summer harvest is almost in. I have an uncle in Rome who comes every year. He usually comes early because the winds are not always dependable, and he would rather lose his right arm than miss even one hour of Pentecost. I've been counting and it's already forty-seven days since Passover!"

In reply to these questions one of the Twelve must have answered: "Jesus didn't say how long. He merely said, 'stay in the city until you've been clothed with power from on high' " (Luke 24:49, NIV).

As the 120 waited, more and more of Jesus' words came back to them. This was as Jesus had prophesied in the Upper Room: "But the Comforter, which is the Holy Ghost, whom the Father will send in my name, he shall teach you *all* things, and bring all things to your *remembrance, whatsoever I have said unto you*" (John 14:26).

As they waited and prayed and studied the Scriptures and shared experiences, the hours slowly meandered by and the Old City continued to fill with pilgrims. Distance meant nothing to those in the Dispersion who wanted to attend Pentecost.

Families in Rome didn't hesitate to board ship even though Jerusalem was nearly fifteen hundred miles away and they had to sleep and eat on deck; nor did the others mind: those who journeyed from Crete, deep in Arabia, Egypt, Pontus, Pamphilia, Libya, Media, and other distant places.

Using all sorts of transportation, pilgrims poured in from all over the known world. Some were mounted on camels, others bumped along in carts; many rode on mules or horses. Some even walked.

As the city filled with visitors, Peter got more and more nervous. But even while he glanced around, the exact words of Jesus began to stream more and more clearly back to him. This was amazing, for those words were now as clear as when Jesus first uttered them. He had often wondered how a blind man felt after he had been healed by Jesus. Now he knew! And not only did he remember Jesus' words; he also remembered the place where he spoke them.

No one, of course, knows, the memories that captivated the minds of the 120 as the Day of Pentecost drew near. But I can imagine Peter remembering the occasion when he said to Jesus. "Lord, how many times shall I forgive my brother when he sins against me? Up to seven times?" (Matt. 18:21, NIV). He also remembered Jesus' instant response, "I tell you not seven times, but seventy-seven times" (v. 22, NIV).

That remembrance was a relief, for he had only gone to sleep in the Garden three times, denied him three times—and used his sword once. *Yes, the Lord could, and had forgiven him!*

Stretching our imaginations a little farther, we can hear and visualize Nicodemus saying: "I will never forget the time I interviewed Jesus on the rooftop. While I was still puzzled about how I could be born again, Jesus said to me, 'Just as Moses lifted up the snake in the desert (Num. 21:8-9), so the Son of Man must be lifted up, that everyone who believes in him may have eternal life' " (John 3:14-15, NIV).

As Peter listened to this man who had helped prepare the body of Jesus for the tomb, his lines of worry gave way to a smile of confidence; and, at the same time, he knew that Jesus had often said:

> For God so loved the world that he gave his one and only Son, that whoever believes in him shall not perish but have eternal life (John 3:16, NIV).

In response to these memories, Peter's confidence returned until it was infinitely stronger than it had been when he dragged in the nets filled with 153 fish. Even so, he felt as bound as Lazarus had felt after he had been raised from the dead.

Although Lazarus was alive, he was still bound and had to wait until at the command of Jesus some of those nearby loosed his grave clothes and freed him from their restraining power.

Can you answer?
1. How long were the eleven disciples to remain in Jerusalem?
2. How long did Jesus remain on earth after his resurrection.
3. Where did Jesus' ascension take place?
4. About how many tarried in Jerusalem awaiting power from on high?
5. Why does Campbell Morgan believe that those who waited, waited in the temple rather than in the Upper Room?
6. Who were the candidates who sought to fill the place of Judas among the Twelve?
7. In what season was the Feast of Pentecost celebrated?

10

Pentecost!

As the sun splashed on the horizon in the west, Peter knew that the day of Pentecost had come. He, along with the other members of the 120, had been waiting for the promised power nearly ten days; and yet nothing of outstanding significance had happened to a single one of them.

Inwardly, Peter may have felt disappointment. It is easy to imagine him rehearsing the command of Jesus: "Do not leave Jerusalem, but wait for the gift my Father promised, which you have heard me speak about. For John baptized with water, but in a few days you will be baptized with the Holy Spirit" (Acts 1:4-5, NIV).

True, the words of Jesus had come alive in his heart; he had been assured that his sins had been forgiven, and he was unusually happy because of that. But as far as a sudden surge of power was concerned, he had neither felt nor seen any evidence of it. He was still like the resurrected Lazarus before he escaped his graveclothes. Nonetheless, he kept busy praying, studying the Septuagint, discussing the work of the Lord with the others—and watching as priests prepared for the forthcoming feast.

Being scrupulously careful to follow the directions of Moses outlined in Numbers 28:26-31, they had arranged to have on hand to be sacrificed as a burnt offering "two young bulls, one ram and seven male lambs a year old as an aroma pleasing to the Lord" (v. 27). In addition, on the day before Pentecost, the authorities had asked the people to bring in their choice sheaves of grain from the wheat harvest.

The grain for the unleavened bread at the Passover was barley. But the grain to be made into bread at the "wave-offering" at Pentecost was wheat. The instructions about how to prepare the two "wave-loaves" was a little complicated; but the instructions were followed as carefully as a modern housewife follows a coveted recipe from her grandmother's cookbook. The recipe in our own words was as follows:

> Three pecks and three pints of wheat should be threshed in the temple . . . and passed through twelve sieves. From the flour thus obtained two omers [about five quarts] (double the quantity used at Passover) should be prepared.
>
> The flour for each loaf must be taken separately and kneaded with lukewarm water in the manner of all thank-offerings, and baked by itself in the temple.
>
> Each loaf should be shaped as follows: It should be seven feet long, four fingers high, four handbreadths wide. Also, the ends and edges should be turned up.
>
> *It is extremely important that these loaves be made the evening before Pentecost.*

As the 120 remained seated, they watched the priests wave the loaves and first-fruits before the Lord, smelled the smoke of the sacrifice, heard the flutes—and listened as the masses sang the Great Hallel.

Suddenly after the morning sun had lighted the streets of Jerusalem there was a mysterious sound. It was "like the blowing of a violent wind . . . from heaven. . . . [It] filled the whole house where they were sitting" (Acts 2:2, NIV).

This sound was mysterious because although it was like "a violent wind," it did not uproot trees, rustle gowns, or even cause people to hold onto their hats. Actually, it was *not* a wind at all. It merely *sounded* like a wind. But knowing that it came from God, Luke described it as "coming from heaven."

Following the wind "there appeared unto them cloven tongues like as of fire, and it sat upon each of them" (v. 3, KJV). This was an eye-boggling sight, for the nonburning flame sat on each of the entire group that had been waiting. It sat on each of the Twelve, including Matthias; and it sat on *all* the others whom Luke had named: Mary, the mother of Jesus, and his brothers. In addition, and without discrimination, it also sat on the heads of all those who had not been named.

If the man who had been possessed of demons from Gadara was there, a flame sat on his head. If the widow who cast two mites into the treasury was there, it sat on her head; and if Simon of Cyrene was there, the flame of fire sat on his head.

Not one of the 120 was neglected!

As the 120 flames trembled over the heads of those who were sitting, another unusual phenomenon took place. This is how Luke recorded that phenomenon in Acts 2:4 according to the NIV:

> All of them were filled with the Holy Spirit and began to speak in other tongues as the Spirit enabled them.

Before we continue with the story about how they all spoke in tongues, it is extremely important that we observe one vital aspect of this entire situation. When a skilled writer wants to emphasize an extremely important point, she or he may make a point come alive to the reader by referring to all five senses. On this occasion, this was skillfully done by the guidance of the Holy Spirit. Notice:

1. The 120 *heard*. "Suddenly a sound like the blowing of a violent wind came from heaven and filled the whole house where they were sitting" (Acts 2:2, NIV).

2. The 120 *saw*. "They saw what seemed to be tongues of fire that separated and came to rest on each of them" (v. 3). In addition to this, the blood-stained stipes-upright-post-of the cross on which Jesus had died, was still standing. That is, it was still standing if normal Roman customs were followed. A glance at the map of Jerusalem in *At the Tomb* (Ludwig 1989) will show that Golgotha was less than half a mile from the temple. Moreover, all of them had undoubtedly seen that post that like an uplifted finger pointed heavenward.

3. The sense of *smell*. This was fulfilled by the smoke from the altar where the animals had been sacrificed.

4. The sense of *touch*. We are made aware of this by Luke who informed his readers that the 120 were *sitting* when they were "filled with the Holy Spirit and began to speak in tongues" (v. 4).

5. The sense of *taste*. This was undoubtedly fulfilled by the abundant harvest Israel had enjoyed, demonstrated by the firstfruits that had been brought in.

We must now delve a little deeper into the unusual facts that took place on this occasion: The sound of "a violent wind"; "the tongues of fire"; and the speaking "in other tongues."

If Nicodemus was one of the 120, as I have suggested, the sound, like "a violent wind," would certainly have brought a comment from him. I can almost hear him saying: "As we sat on the roof and a soft wind tugged at our gowns, Jesus said: 'The wind blows *wherever* it pleases. You hear its sound, but you cannot tell where it comes from or where it is going. *So it is with everyone born of the Spirit*' " (John 3:8, NIV).

The mystery of the sound of "a violent wind" that didn't rustle a single gown will never be solved. But a clue to at least one of its purposes come to us through the words of Jesus: "The wind blows wherever it pleases."

This clue indicates that the Holy Spirit like a wind or a dove moves *wherever* and *however* God wills for it to move.

The roaring sound of this "violent wind" that didn't even stir the dust must have reminded every listener of Ezekiel's experience with the dry bones. This story was one they had heard and enjoyed from the time they were children:

> The hand of the Lord was upon me [wrote Ezekiel], and he brought me out by the Spirit of the Lord and set me in the middle of a valley; it was full of bones. He led me back and forth among them, and I saw a great many bones on the floor of the valley, bones that were very dry. He asked me, "Son of man, can these bones live?"
> I said, "O Sovereign Lord, you alone know."
> Then he said to me, "Prophesy to these bones and say to them, 'Dry bones, hear the word of the Lord! This is what the Sovereign Lord says to these bones: I will make breath enter you, and you will come to life. I will attach tendons to you and make flesh come upon you and cover you with skin; I will put breath in you, and you will come to life. Then you will know that I am Lord.' "
> So I prophesied as I was commanded. And as I was prophesying, there was a noise, a rattling sound, and the bones came together, bone to bone. I looked, and tendons and flesh appeared on them, but there was no breath in them.
> Then he said to me, "Prophesy to the breath; prophesy, son of man, and say to it, 'This is what the Sovereign Lord says: Come from the four winds, O breath, and breathe into these slain, that they may live.' " So I prophesied as he commanded me, and breath entered them; they came to life and stood up on their feet—a vast army.
> Then he said to me: "Son of man, these bones are the whole house of Israel" (Ezekiel 37:1-11, NIV).

As the sound of the violent, nonexistent wind moaned and whistled in their midst, did the 120 wonder if they personally were the dry bones in the valley of dry bones? No one knows, but surely their eyes must have filled with wonder as they nervously glanced at one another. Moreover, each one, whether fisher, carpenter, bookkeeper, widow, rich, or poor, was utterly convinced that he or she was needed by God and was a vital part of God's plan.

The tongues of fire are filled with additional mystery. In the New International Version we have a slight variation from the KJV where Acts 2:3 reads: "There appeared unto them cloven tongues like as of fire." That variation states: "They saw what seemed to be tongues of fire that *separated* and came to rest on each of them."

The variation that the tongues of fire had been *one*, that they *separated* and rested on each of the 120, is also maintained in J. B. Phillip's translation: "Before their eyes appeared tongues like flames, which *separated off* and settled on the head of each one of them."

This sense of the *oneness* of the Holy Spirit is extremely important to us, especially when we remember that Luke wrote: "When the day of Pentecost was fully come, they were all with *one* accord in *one* place" (v. 1, KJV).

Another facet about the tongues of fire is that they remind one of the flame in the burning bush. As Moses stood watching the strange flame that did not crackle or consume the bush, the Lord spoke from the bush and said: "I have indeed seen the misery of my people in Egypt . . . I have come down to rescue them from the hand of the Egyptians. . . . So now, go, I am sending you to Pharaoh to bring my people . . . out of Egypt" (Exodus 3:7-10, NIV).

This facet shouts with drama. Instead of seeing *a burning bush, they*, all of them, *were* burning bushes! And, instead of asking them to lead slaves from slavery, they, all of them, were being asked to take the Good News of Jesus Christ to the entire world! This fact burned in their hearts for many of them had heard Jesus personally say: "All authority in heaven and on earth has been given to me. Therefore go and make disciples of all nations, baptizing him in the name of the Father and of the Son and of the Holy Spirit" (Matt. 28:18-19, NIV).

The word *fire* has numerous facets. John the Baptist was categorical. He said: "I baptize you with water for repentance. But after me will come one who is more powerful than I whose sandals I am not fit to carry. He will baptize you with the Holy Spirit, *and with fire*" (Matthew 3:11).

Malachi indicated a meaning of divine fire: "[Jesus] will be like a refiner's fire" (v. 3:2).

Again, each one, whether a fisher, carpenter, bookkeeper, rich, or poor, was convinced that he or she was needed by God and was a vital part of God's plan. Jesus had underlined this by asking the seven disciples at the lake to provide extra fish when he prepared breakfast!

The sounds of "a violent wind" and the "tongues of fire" were not the end of the Pentecostal experience; for, in addition, "All of them were filled with the Holy Spirit and began to speak in other tongues as the Spirit enabled them" (Acts 2:4).

The word *tongues, glossolalia* in Greek, although so rendered in the NEB and RSV, is not always translated tongues. J. B. Phillips rendered the passage: "They were all filled with the Holy Spirit and began to speak in different *languages* as the Spirit gave them power to proclaim his message."

Whether *glossolalia* should be translated "languages" or "tongues" is a mute point. This is indicated by the fact that the crowd

> came together in bewilderment, because each one heard them speaking in his *own language*. Utterly amazed, they asked: "Are not all these men who are speaking Galilean? Then how is it that each of us hears them in his own native language? Parthians, Medes and Elamites; residents of Mesopotamia, Judea and Cappadocia, Pontus and Asia, Phyrgia and Pamphylia, Egypt and parts of Libya near Cyrene; visitors from Rome (both Jews and converts to Judaism); Cretans and Arabs—we hear them declaring the wonders of God in our own tongues!" Amazed and perplexed, they asked one another, "What does this mean?"

Some, however, made fun of them and said, "They have had too much wine" (Acts 2:6-13, NIV).

Studying this in perspective, we ask a number of questions: Why did the 120 speak in other languages when, undoubtedly, at least most of the listeners understood Greek, the *lingua franca* of all the nations involved.

1. One answer is that since this was the birthday of the Church, it was imperative for the entire world to know that the Church, the body of Christ, was for *all* races, *all* languages, *all* nations, *all* cultures, and *all* levels of society.

2. Another answer is that the Lord wanted the entire group to be assured that they had been baptized with the Holy Spirit.

3. An additional reason was that because of the many languages spoken, especially by those who did not normally speak them, the masses were drawn to the 120 and were thoroughly impressed.

After some had accused the 120 of being drunk, Peter leaped to his feet and began to preach the first sermon he had ever preached.

The gift of being able to preach a sermon that wins masses to Christ is a rare gift and one that is possessed by only a chosen few. Henry Ward Beecher, the son of the famous Lyman Beecher, one of America's great preachers, and president of Lane Seminary, felt certain that he had this gift. But Sunday after Sunday as he preached in his first church at Lawrenceburgh, Indiana, all of his sermons fell flat. Few even listened.

Determined to remedy the situation, Beecher made a study of the recorded sermons in the New Testament. He soon discovered that the apostles began their sermons by speaking about that which was known and understood by their hearers, and then branching into the unknown. This was the method of the greatest of all preachers, Jesus Christ himself.

Experimenting with this method, Beecher wrote a sermon that started with the known and then ventured into the unknown. The result was that many were converted, and he was so overwhelmed by his success, he kept repeating to himself: "I've learned to preach! I've learned to preach!"

Beecher's first model was Jesus Christ himself. In Jesus' famed sermon preached while he was sitting at the edge of the well in Samaria (John 4:5-29), Jesus, after his introduction, began his message by stating a very obvious fact: "Everyone who drinks this water will be thirsty again" (v. 13). Then he continued with an unknown fact: "Whoever drinks the water that I will give him will never thirst. Indeed the water I give him will become in him a spring of water welling up to eternal life" (4:13-14, NIV).

Other than by example, there is no evidence that Jesus ever gave his disciples a single lesson in homiletics. Even so, inspired by the Holy Spirit, Peter preached in the same way in which Jesus had preached. Notice:

His introduction was gripping. It explained that he was one of them: "*Fellow* Jews and all of you who live in Jerusalem, let me explain this to you; listen carefully to what I say" (2:14).

Next, he spoke about that which they all knew. He started with a long quotation from Joel, a book with which they were all familiar. Then in a diplomatic way, he began to probe to the quick: "Men of Israel, listen to this: Jesus of Nazareth was a man accredited by God to work miracles, wonders, and signs, which God did among you through him, as you yourself know."

At this point, although still diplomatic, Peter proceeded to slice deeper and deeper into the quick: "This man was handed to you by God's set purpose and foreknowledge; and you, with the help of wicked men [ouch!], put him to death by nailing him to the cross. But God raised him from the dead, freeing him from the agony of death, because it was impossible for death to keep its hold on him."

Following this statement, Peter in the manner of Jesus, made his statement extremely relevant by referring to David. Visitors to Jerusalem know that David was buried near the Upper Room where Jesus celebrated his Last Supper with the Twelve.

Having intensified their attention, Peter then began to expound the very heart of the gospel:

> Brothers, I can tell you confidently that the patriarch David died and was buried, and his tomb is here to this day. But he was a prophet and knew that God had promised him on oath that he would place one of his descendants on his throne [Psalm 132:11]. Seeing what was ahead, he spoke of the resurrection of the Christ, that he was not abandoned to the grave, nor did his body see decay [Psalm 16:10]. God has raised this Jesus to life, and we are all witnesses of that fact. Exalted to the right hand of God, he has received from the Father the promised Holy Spirit and has poured out what you now see and hear (Acts 2:22-37).

As he spoke, Peter was aware of the convicting power of the Holy Spirit within the masses. He then eased in the net after he had exhorted: "Repent and be baptized, every one of you" (v. 38).

What kind of response did Peter get? "Those who accepted his message were baptized, and about three thousand were added to their number that day" (v. 41).

At the conclusion of Pentecost, the visitors from abroad returned to their homes; and the church continued to expand. Glowing reports are scattered through the Book of Acts: "The Lord added daily to their number" (v. 47). "Many who heard the message believed, and the number of men grew to about five thousand" (4:4). "Believers were the more added to the Lord, multitudes of both men and women" (5:14, KJV). "The word of the Lord grew and multiplied" (12:24).

In addition, many were healed.

> The apostles performed many signs and wonders among the people. . . . As a result, people brought the sick into the streets and laid them on beds and

mats so that at least Peter's shadow might fall on some of them as he passed by.... Crowds gathered also from the towns around Jerusalem, bringing their sick and those tormented by evil spirits, *and all of them were healed* (5:12, 15, 16).

These facts prove that Jesus was right when after the Last Supper he said: "I tell you the truth, *anyone* who has faith in me will do what I have been doing. He will do even greater things than these, because I am going to the Father" (John 14:12).

Inspired by their baptism in the Holy Spirit and fire, the 120, the fishers, carpenters, bookkeepers, widows, rich, and poor spread throughout Jerusalem. They knocked on doors, broke bread, and relayed the way of salvation and what they had experienced to others. All of them believed intensely that Jesus' promise, "He that believeth on me, the works that I do shall he do also; and greater works than these shall he do; because I go unto my Father" included each one of them.

Can you answer?
1. How long had the 120 tarried in Jerusalem before they were baptized with the Holy Spirit?
2. What Scriptures did the group who tarried in Jerusalem have available for study?
3. In what ways did the Day of Pentecost appeal to all five human senses?
4. What grain was used to make the bread that would be waved before the Lord?
5. How did the tongues of fire remind people of Moses?
6. What is the Greek word for tongues?
7. How many were added to the Church of God on the Day of Pentecost?

11

The Holy Spirit's Ministry

Curiously, one of the most vital works of the Holy Spirit is that of closing doors. Moreover, the Holy Spirit does not always close them gently. On occasions he slams them. Bang! Just like that.

Experienced followers of Christ, however, have learned that a closed door generally means an open door to another field. All Christians remember Bithynia. No, Luke didn't say the Holy Spirit slammed the door in Paul's face. Instead, he wrote: "When they came to the border of Mysia, they tried to enter Bithynia, but the Spirit of Jesus would not allow them to" (Acts 16:7, NIV).

Not being permitted to enter Bithynia must have been a keen disappointment to Paul. Warmed by the Black Sea, Bithynia was a coveted place in which to work and live. (The Russians have made it into a coveted vacation spot!) But the Holy Spirit said no. Nonetheless, at the very time that Bithynia was closed to him, a wide door was opened to Macedonia.

But in this dispensation of grace does the Holy Spirit still close and open doors? The answer is: he certainly does. During my own lifetime there were periods when it seemed to me that slamming doors in my face was someone's specialty. Still, I'm not the only one who has felt that way.

Twenty-year-old Phillips Brooks was as certain that fate

was closing doors in his face as he was that his father was a hardware merchant and that they lived in Boston.

Phillips was handsome. He was just under six feet four inches tall; and since he loved foreign languages and had a brilliant mind, he studied hard in order to teach Latin.

But when he faced his students, he was dismayed to learn that they loathed him. They had demolished the previous four teachers and because of Phillips' size they considered him an appropriate target. They persecuted him in every way their cruel minds could imagine.

They locked him in his room, scattered explosive matches across the classroom floor, and hurled buckshot in his face.

Brokenhearted, he wailed in a letter to an acquaintance: "[I don't] recall a single teacher who was honored with such an overwhelming share of deep, steady, honest unpopularity as is at this moment the lot of your harmless and inoffensive friend."

His teaching career lasted two weeks!

When a former schoolmate called at his home, Phillips' father was frank: "[He] will not see anyone now, but after he is over his feeling of mortification, he will come and see you."

Eventually the humiliated Latin teacher felt his call to the ministry and enrolled in the Virginia Theological Seminary. Swallowing the slur that anyone who failed at teaching could not possibly succeed at anything, Phillips studied hard and became more and more convinced that God had called him to the ministry.

Last October when I visited Trinity Church in Boston and visualized the throngs that packed it to the doors when Phillips Brooks was its pastor, I was profoundly thankful that he had failed as a teacher.

Moreover, this feeling of mine is shared by additional millions every Christmas season when we sing his always famous "O Little Town of Bethlehem."

Today his sermonic masterpieces are studied—and preached!—by thousands. His greatest gift, however, was neither in homiletics nor hymn writing. (He read his sermons and spoke so rapidly he was the despair of stenographers).

His greatest gift, a very subtle gift, was expressed to him in a highly prized letter from a man who worked near his church in Copley Square:

"Dear Mr. Brooks: I am a tailor near your Church. Whenever I have the opportunity I always go to hear you preach. Each time I hear you preach I seem to forget you, for you make me think of God."

Other well-knowns who faced closed doors are David Livingstone, E. Stanley Jones—and Peter Marshall. Curiously, all three of them felt called to be missionaries in China. And yet, as we study their lives, we realize that David Livingstone was *the* man for Africa. E. Stanley Jones was *the* man for India—and Peter Marshall was *the* man for the New York Avenue Presbyterian Church in Washington, D.C.

The one who opens and closes the doors in our lives never makes mistakes, and he always does that which is best for both us and the world!

Modern science informs us that if the DNA in our bodies were uncoiled it could stretch the 93 million miles to the sun *and* back 400 times. Furthermore, Dr. Paul Brand estimates that if all the instructions in our DNA were written out, they would fill 1,600 page books. Because of this, he wrote: "A nerve cell may operate according to instructions from volume four and a kidney cell from volume twenty-five" (Brand and Yancey 45-46).

Those figures are so far beyond us we cannot comprehend them, but the Holy Spirit understands each of the instructions in our DNA. Furthermore, the Spirit understands all of the spiritual gifts that are available to endow each Spirit-filled person. Likewise, the spirit is anxious to endow each one with a gift or gifts according to our needs. Many gifts are mentioned in the New Testament. An excellent list to start with is the entire twelfth chapter of First Corinthians.

The word *gift* or *gifts* appears fifty times in the RSV!

Since all of the above is scripturally correct, should any of us be overly concerned when the door we had hoped to enter is slammed and bolted in our faces?

At the conclusion of Peter's Pentecostal sermon, "the people were cut to the heart and said to Peter and the other apostles, 'Brothers, what shall we do?' " (Acts 2:37, NIV). This passage indicates that the Holy Spirit was faithfully working. The function of the Spirit in condemning us of sin is so important that all humankind was warned long ago in Genesis 6:3, "Then the Lord said, 'My Spirit will not abide in mortals forever' " (NRSV).

The Holy Spirit's work in pointing out sin continues and is felt in all types and classes of people. Because of this Paul warned: "Do not grieve the Holy Spirit" (Eph. 4:30, NIV).

Although Beethoven is not remembered as a spiritual giant, he did acknowledge his love of God when he exclaimed: "I owe it to myself and to mankind and to the Almighty . . . I must write my music . . . to the eternal glory of God." Thus inspired, he wrote glorious parts that contemporary instruments could not play. When chided for this he answered with a question: "Do you believe that I think of a wretched fiddle when the spirit speaks to me?"

Although he gradually became stone deaf, Beethoven did not allow his handicap to hinder him. Instead, he finished the Ninth without being able to hear a single note. But in spite of his virtues, this stubby man with a swarthy face had a caustic tongue. Did the Holy Spirit ever speak to him? Certainly! Consider this letter that Beethoven wrote to his friend Dr. Wegeler:

> Dearest! Best!
> In what an odious light you have exhibited me to myself! I acknowledge it, I do not deserve your friendship . . . but thank heaven, it was no intentional or deliberate malice which induced me to act as I did toward you. It was my inexcusable thoughtlessness which prevented me from seeing the matter in its true light. . . . Ah, Wegeler, do not reject this hand of reconciliation . . . I am coming to throw myself into your arms. . . . Pray give your-

self back to me, your penitent, loving, never-forgetting friend.

Ludwig Van Beethoven

(Thomas and Thomas 74-75)

Experienced believers rejoice when they feel the sharp pricks of the Holy Spirit. The rebukes of the Spirit indicate that they are alive and that the Holy Spirit longs for their improvement. Although the wasteful son lost everything, he remained sensitive to the rebukes and wooing of the Holy Spirit; and this provided him with a joyous homecoming.

Realizing the problems that would be faced by the Seventy, Jesus was extremely candid. "Go!" he said. "I am sending you out like lambs among wolves" (Luke 10:3, NIV). Since this is still a fact, one of the assignments of the Holy Spirit is to comfort every worker in the Kingdom.

An illustration of his comforting power is revealed to us in one of the diaries of David Livingstone.

Following years of separation brought about by his journeys of discovery, David's wife, Mary, returned from Scotland to be with him. She had only been there a short time when she was stricken with illness. On April 21 she fell into a coma and was immediately rushed to the House in Shupanga not far from Africa's famed Zambesi. (He had been exploring this river in order to open an easy entrance for missionaries to penetrate the interior).

As he sat near her rude bed formed of boxes, his mind kept going over their many years together. He remembered their courting days in Kuruman, the way she taught the girls in the little school, the dark days when she suffered partial paralysis of her face; the time they lost their oldest child. (She was, he wrote in his diary "a sweet little girl with blue eyes. . . . We could not apply remedies to one so young. . . . She uttered a piercing cry, and then went away to see the King in His beauty."

While the past stirred before him, he did what he could to help Mary to be as comfortable as possible. Realizing that the time was near, he sent for Dr. Stewart, the one who gave the world this classic paragraph of those last heartrending moments:

> The man who had faced so many deaths, and braved so many dangers, was now utterly broken down and weeping like a child. I found my own eyes were full. . . . He asked me to commit her soul to her Maker. . . . He, Dr. Kirk kneeled down and I prayed as best I could. In less than an hour she was gone.

After she had been buried near a "large baobab" tree, David Livingstone again confided to his diary:

> It is the first heavy stroke I have suffered, and it quite takes away my strength. I wept over her who well deserved many tears. God pity the children.

But Jesus did not forsake him; for, as he promised, he had provided him with "another Comforter" (John 14:16, KJV). From additional notes in his diary we can see how the Holy Spirit continued to work:

> 11th May. My dear, dear Mary has been this evening a fortnight in heaven—absent from the body present with the Lord. . . . For the first time in my life I feel willing to die.—D.L.
> 19th May. Vividly do I remember my first passage down in 1856 passing Shupanga House. . . . No suspicion glanced across my mind that my loving wife would be called to give up the ghost six years afterward. . . .
> 31st May. She was ready and anxious to work, but has been called away to serve God in a higher sphere.

As we read the diary, undoubtedly inspired by the Holy Spirit, we notice by Livingstone's own words that the Comforter was slowly brightening his eyes. The final proof of this is that instead of retiring to Scotland after Mary's death, enjoying his fame, and being with his children, he continued to exhort from the bed on which he was being carried, as one of his last porters, Matthew Wellington, repeated to me: "Twende! Twende! (Let us go on. Let us go on.")

The Holy Spirit had assigned him tasks to perform and he was determined not to rest until he had fulfilled each task.

But the Holy Spirit does more than lead and comfort and inspire; the Spirit also demands and motivates. Our minds skip back to the scene at the Feast of Tabernacles in chapter 1 where, instead of giving a lesson in hygiene, a lesson that would have saved thousands of lives, Jesus said: "If anyone is thirsty, let him come to me and drink. Whoever believes in me, as the Scripture has said, *streams of living water will flow from within him*" (John 7:38, NIV).

A major reason for this is undoubtedly because "God created humankind in his own image" (1:27, NRSV); and since God is creative, God longs for us to be creative. This means that just as parents rejoice when their children achieve a breakthrough, as insignificant as the breakthrough may be, God rejoices when human beings achieve breakthroughs—especially breakthroughs that help God's children.

Sir Albert Cook underlined this fact.

Arriving in Mombasa in 1896, Dr. Cook along with fifteen other missionaries walked the six hundred miles to what became Kampala in Uganda. There he set up his medical practice while he continued to serve the Lord in a spiritual way. After he had operated on a settler, he sat by his side and asked: "Are you, my friend, saved?"

"Certainly," smiled the man, "and you saved me."

"Oh, I don't mean your corporal body," replied Cook. "I mean your immortal soul."

This slender Church of England missionary made use of every second and every useful help he could find. Some of his helpers were strange indeed. Friday, from dawn to dusk, was his operating day. What did he do with the arm or leg he had amputated? He ordered it placed under a tree where a vulture returned every Friday to dispose of it.

The vulture was quite efficient.

Cook did everything possible to discover ways to obliterate tropical diseases that were killing tens of thousands. Although lacking the equipment of a research scientist, he made use of what he could find. Old wine bottles became retorts, and a charcoal flame fanned by a native took the place of a Bunsen burner.

By means of this crude equipment, he discovered that relapsing fever is carried by a certain wood tick. Also he identified the worm responsible for anemia, and he made great advances in the control of one of Uganda's worst diseases—sleeping sickness.

One of the bright spots in my life was when I visited the hospital where Dr. Cook served during his lifetime, and I remember vividly when King George V bestowed upon him a well-deserved knighthood.

In the manner of Sir Albert, other missionaries such as Paul Brand have made great advances toward the eventual eradication of leprosy and other scourges that have terrified humankind.

What inspired them? *Rivers of living water!*

These refreshing rivers have motivated others in many diverse fields. John Dalton, the Quaker who developed the atomic theory, was a spirit-filled man, and so was Isaac Newton, the discoverer of the laws of gravity. Michael Faraday, the Sandemanian elder and lay preacher who believed in foot washing, proved that magnetism could be changed into electricity. In addition, he invented the electric generator.

Ah, but we must not forget Nikolaus Copernicus, the son of a poor Polish baker who revolutionized our thinking by informing the world that the earth moves around the sun. Such an idea was dark heresy. Heretics during his lifetime—

1473 to 1543—were burned at the stake.

Copernicus—the name was originally *Kopirnig*, which means *humble*, researched his ideas and wrote them out in a book. But having no desire to be burned alive, he kept the manuscript hidden for thirty-six years. Finally persuaded to have it published, he diplomatically dedicated it to Pope Paul III, and entrusted it to his friend Tidemann Gysius, bishop of Culm, to see it through the press.

The bent researcher was on his deathbed when the book was handed to him. As he eagerly read it, he noticed that an unknown, apparently fearing for the safety of the author, had included a line designed to at least partially protect the author from an awaiting stake. The line read: "This book was written to present not a scientific fact but a playful fancy."

What did Doctor Copernicus do for a living? He was a Catholic priest! His Ph.D. was in canon law. What inspired him to risk his life by publishing such a heretical book? *Rivers of living water!*

One of the words that bristles in the works of John Wesley is *providence*. In our time that word is practically forgotten. We seldom hear it, even in church. This is a pity, for one of the most effective tools used by the Holy Spirit is providence.

Why was the Mayflower twice blown off course and thus unable to reach Jamestown where the Pilgrims had a charter from King James? Providence! (Had they landed in Jamestown, they would have still been governed by him. But by landing at what became known as Provincetown Harbor, they were inspired to adopt the Mayflower Compact and become the first democracy in America).

Why didn't Hitler invade Britain in the summer of 1940 when the Island Kingdom only had one hundred rusty tanks? Had he done so he might have won the war. Providence! Why does the Lord often guide Christian writers to the right book when they are doing research? Providence!

Why is the right doctor often available at just the time when it means life or death? Providence!

That providence is a reality is proved by the fact that

altogether, including *Provedeniya* in the Soviet Union, there are fifteen areas in the world whose names are either Providence or are derived from the word providence.

Madam Ernestine Schumann-Heink had many *human* reasons to be discouraged. Her husband had left her; and, according to German law, she had to repay his debts. Since she was poverty-stricken, the sheriff seized all her furniture with the exception of their bed and a chair.

So pressed was she for money that she accepted an invitation to sing just six hours before she went into labor with her youngest child. Ernestine was a thorough Christian. She prayed on her knees every morning and every night, and she read the Bible daily. Even so, hungry and shivering in a cold room, she decided that her best move was to commit suicide.

After gathering her children, she led them to the railway tracks where she planned to hurl them and then herself in front of a speeding train. But just as the train was approaching her little girl grabbed her skirts and cried, "Mama, I love you. It's so cold. Please let's go home!"

Startled by what she had almost done, Ernestine hurried her children back to the cold room. Her struggles continued, but eventually Madam Schumann-Heink made her over-the-top debut and became famous as one of the world's greatest opera singers. Fans stood in line at the Metropolitan in New York, the Royal Opera House in Berlin, and Covent Garden in London to hear her star in Beethoven's Ninth, Wagner's *Lohengrin*, and other classics.

What inspired the little girl to cry, "Mama. I love you. It's so cold. Please, let's go home!" at just the right time? Providence!

All who viewed the 120 when they were baptized with the Holy Spirit and witnessed the conversion of the three thousand in one service were not impressed.

Those in power were convinced the movement could not possibly last. Moreover, those who understood human nature had good reason to feel that way. One can imagine the high priest dismissing the new movement with a wave and sneering: "Those who survive the Romans and the stones of the masses will be paralyzed by jealousy.

"I've already heard that the mother of James and John went to Jesus and asked that one of her sons sit on his right and the other on his left when he came into his kingdom!" The high priest shook his head. And later, when the other ten members of the group heard about this they almost foamed with jealousy. Jealousy, the worst disease of the human race will get them" (See Matt. 20:20-24).

Jealousy is indeed a potent disease. It destroys families, churches, missions, nations. How could the Twelve escape being ruined by that insidious disease?

Let's pause and study the differences between Saul of Tarsus and Simon Peter, the two likeliest candidates to be neutralized by jealousy toward one another. Both had strong personalities. But whereas Peter had merely hacked off a man's ear, Saul had murdered Christians; and whereas Saul was a highly educated man, Peter was merely a fisherman.

Insisting that due to the suicide of Judas their number should be restored to twelve, Peter made the speech that this should be done while the 120 tarried in Jerusalem. After casting lots, the lot favored Matthias and made him number twelve. But having changed his name from Saul to Paul, the murderer from Tarsus insisted that he, too, was an apostle! (Romans 1:1 and 11:13).

That claim must have been like ground glass in Peter's eyes, for the number twelve was an important number. Jacob had *twelve* sons; there were *twelve* tribes; and Solomon chose *twelve* governors to rule the *twelve* districts of Israel. Indeed, altogether, the number twelve is mentioned nearly one hundred times in the Old Testament! But as disagreeable as that may have been to Peter, there were other problems that were undoubtedly even more disagreeable.

While in Antioch Peter had associated and eaten with Gentiles; but after a committee arrived from James, Peter refused to eat with Gentiles. This changing of priorities so aggravated Paul he publicly denounced Peter to his face.

That denunciation from this self-proclaimed apostle was

bad enough. But Paul didn't stop with this single public denunciation. In addition, he wrote in detail about it in his letter to the Galatians (2:11-14). Even worse, copies of that letter were being circulated around in the churches!

While reading a copy of Paul's letter in some distant city, Peter had to pray, and swallow, in order to keep his equilibrium.

Did Peter retaliate? Never! His only published reference to Paul is found in 2 Peter 3:15. There, with generosity, he wrote: "Bear in mind that our Lord's patience means salvation, just as our *dear brother Paul* also wrote you with the wisdom that God gave him." In verse 16 Peter went on to observe that "his letters contain some things that are hard to understand, which ignorant and unstable people distort" (NIV). But at that point all of us will have to agree with Peter.

Still there were formidable problems!

One day John Mark approached Peter with a dilemma. He and Paul had parted; and he, John Mark, had returned to Jerusalem. No one knows the *real* reason why they parted (Acts 13:13), but we do know that Mark began to work with Peter, and that Peter referred to Mark as "my son" (1 Peter 5:13).

Moreover, one surmises that John Mark learned much of the gospel he wrote from Peter. Nonetheless, in spite of the fact that he and Peter were very close, one will not find a single barb aimed at Paul in the Gospel of Mark, even though Mark did note that Peter had denied the Lord! (Mark 14:66-72).

In addition to this remarkable fact, we have some of Paul's final words as recorded in 2 Tim. 4:11—"Only Luke is with me. Take John Mark, and bring him with thee: for he is profitable to me for the ministry."

This is not the final evidence that these giant opposites ignored their differences and got along. Another startling fact is that again and again when Paul referred to Peter in his epistles, he referred to him by his favorite name, Cephas— the Rock!

Why is it that neither Peter nor Paul allowed jealousy to minimize their work? Could it be Peter remembered that as Jesus approached to wash his feet, he remarked "You do not realize now what I am doing, but later you will understand?" (John 13:7, NIV). That may have helped. But *the* final reason for their harmony is that both of them had been baptized with the Holy Spirit!

Can you answer?
1. Where did Paul and his friends go after the Holy Spirit closed the door for their entrance to Bithynia?
2. Who wrote "O Little Town of Bethlehem?"
3. On the Day of Pentecost, each of the five senses of the 120 was appealed to. Name the five senses and the appeal.
4. Name one of the women who was among the 120 at Pentecost.
5. What famous Christian singer planned to commit suicide?
6. Why did the Pilgrims draw up the Mayflower Compact?
7. Name three ways in which Peter and Paul were opposites.

12

The Holy Spirit Baptism Is for *All* Believers!

The limitless power of the Holy Spirit is impossible to comprehend; and our minds reel when we contemplate the extent and purpose of the work of the Spirit.

This third member of the Trinity convicts us; comforts us; leads us; prods us; teaches us; protects us; challenges us; purifies us with fire; speaks to our congregations, our relatives, and those on our prayer lists. The Spirit also motivates us and does countless other work for our edification and benefit.

It is also incredible to realize that this Third Person of the Trinity is omnipresent and omnipotent. When we read in First Corinthians that Paul insisted that our bodies are the temple of the Holy Spirit (3:16), we must bow our heads in humility and adoration.

Contrast the Holy Spirit and his work with a practice of a fanatical group of Muslims in Nigeria. Here's a testimony from a former follower of the Prophet in that country who accepted Christ: "I escaped death, but was forced to drink certain concoctions intended to bring about my reconversion.

"Muslims frequently write verses from the Koran on a slate, then wash the writing off with water, and force someone to drink the residue, believing that the liquid charms the one who drinks it. Sometimes they mix in certain herbs supposed to have magical qualities when incantations are said over them."

(These methods are not used by orthodox Islam. As in other religions, Islam has fanatical, irrational groups).

The truth about the power of the Holy Spirit in our lives is quite beyond us. But a blurring glimpse of his power, love, and effectiveness in his work was brought to my mind a few years ago while I was in England researching my book *Susanna Wesley; Mother of John and Charles*.

Since the cheapest hotel in the little town where we had stopped was full, we were forced to take a room in the most expensive hotel. At breakfast when the waiter learned that I was a writer, he said: "A rather well-known writer used to stop here."

"Yes?"

"You may have heard of him," he replied as he refilled my cup with coffee.

"What was his name?"

"Winston Churchill."

"Churchill!" I exclaimed.

"Yes, Winston Churchill. Came here to hunt."

After I had settled back to earth, I asked, "What room did he stay in?"

"Number one."

"Then why did the manager put us in number six?"

(Years ago when I stopped at a rooming house in New England, the landlady offered a room to Mary and me for ten dollars. The additional six dollars was because King George had slept in the bed. When I hesitated, the thrifty woman led us to another room and pointed to a bed on which Walt Disney had slept. "You can have this one for only eight dollars," she bargained. Still not convinced, we stayed in a regular room for four dollars).

But Winston Churchill had stayed in room number one, and we could have slept in that room for the same price we had paid for number six!

As I drove to London where I was to preach the next day, my mind went back to our visit at Dunkerque where the British Army had been trapped by the Germans. It was there that the Royal Air Force, though outnumbered eight to one, managed to hold the initiative until tiny boats from England rescued their army.

While viewing the gravestones at the little cemetery in Dunkerque, the final resting place of the youthful pilots who gave their lives, my eyes overflowed, and once again I rehearsed the words of Churchill that had become a part of my being:

> Never in the field of human conflict was so much owed by so many to so few.

Then, continuing on toward London, and remembering to keep to the left, I once again heard echoes of the somber voice of Churchill as he addressed the House of Commons:

> The whole fury and might of the enemy must very soon be turned on us. Hitler knows that he will have to break us in this island or lose the war. If we can stand up to him, all Europe may be free and the life of the world may move forward into broad, sunlit uplands. But if we fail, then the whole world, including the United States, including all that we have known and cared for, will sink into the abyss of a new Dark Age, made more sinister by perverted science. Let us therefore brace ourselves to our duties, and so bear ourselves that, if the British Empire and its Commonwealth last for a thousand years, men will still say: "This was their finest hour" (Churchill, 225-226).

"Just think, Mary," I repeated, "if we had known that Winston Churchill had slept in room number one, we might have also stayed in it for the entire night!"

That experience sank into my subconscious. Then a few weeks later when it presented itself to me early one morning, I discovered that it had rearranged itself into a dynamic fact that has been an inspiration ever since.

In the first place, Prime Minister Churchill was wrong

when he said, "Never in the field of human conflict was so much owed by so many to so few." Why? Because the fact is that never before in the history of human conflict was so much owed by so many to such a one—Jesus Christ! Moreover, the one who died for me has come to live in my heart, and I can "sup with him and he with me" (Rev. 3:20).

But that isn't all. He has also made me a "joint heir" (Romans 8:17).

In the second place the prime minister's suggestion that the British Empire and its Commonwealth might last for a thousand years in no way compares to the kingdom of God which will not last for a mere thousand years, nor even a thousand times a thousand years, but will last forever! Better yet, all believers are part of that kingdom. Indeed, we are right now, according to the word of God, "kings and priests" (Rev. 1:6).

Satan, of course, is horrified by the power of Pentecost. The idea that his enemies, the children of God, can be filled with the Spirit, guided by the Spirit, motivated by the Spirit, and cleansed by the Spirit, is utterly devastating. In our time he remembers the devastation that was wrought in his kingdom by the Apostle Paul, the Twelve, and their followers.

Because it is impossible for Satan to overcome the Holy Spirit, and since he longs for *holocaust* rather than Pentecost, he strains to keep believers from having Spirit-filled lives by getting them to quarrel over the gifts, the work, the ultimate purpose of the Holy Spirit, and on and on.

Disagreements about the Holy Spirit center around many points, including the following:
1. Does a believer receive the Holy Spirit at the time of conversion, or later?
2. By what evidence does a believer know that she or he has been baptized by the Holy Spirit?
3. Is it necessary to tarry in order to receive the baptism of the Holy Spirit?
4. Does the baptism of the Holy Spirit—some call it sanctifica-

tion—eradicate a believer from the tendency to sin?
5. Does a believer who has been baptized by the Holy Spirit ever need a fresh anointing?
6. What must one do to receive the baptism of the Holy Spirit?
7. How can we grieve the Holy Spirit?
8. Since the Holy Spirit is a person, how can we have more or less of him?

In that it is not our aim to be dogmatic about a single point of view in regard to this subject, we will, instead, refer to well-knowns who were, and testified to having been, baptized by the Holy Spirit. Also we will indicate clear New Testament signposts.

When Dwight L. Moody was converted in his youth, he shifted his ambition from wanting to accumulate one hundred thousand dollars to that of building an effective Sunday school in Chicago. Following this, he founded and became the pastor of a church in the Windy City.

In 1869 he began to notice "two elderly, Free Methodist women in frail health" who came to his prayer meetings in Farwell Hall. He soon learned that their names were Mrs. Cooke and Mrs. Snow.

Concerned because they always seemed to be glancing in his direction and then closing their eyes in prayer, he approached them in order to learn the nature of the obvious burden they were carrying.

"We're praying for you," they admitted. "We're convinced that you're not in the will of God, nor are you filled with the Spirit!"

Their answer was a shocker; for, if he was not in the will of God, why did he have the largest congregation in Chicago? But he could not forget those "dreadful women," especially after one of them laid her hand on his shoulder and said, "Lad, Jehovah is dealing with thee!"

Startled, Moody invited them to his house. There, they showed him by the Scriptures that God's plan was for all God's children to be baptized with the Holy Spirit.

Shortly after this, the city of Chicago, including Moody's church, burned. Moody fled to Brooklyn to raise money to rebuild. While there, he continued to think about the words of Mrs. Snow and Mrs. Cooke. Being well-known, he was invited to preach in various places, but somehow he felt that his messages were wooden, uninspired. Then one night in November as he was walking down the street, he sobbed out a *new* prayer from the depths of his heart: "Oh God, why don't you *compel* me to walk close to thee, always? Deliver me from myself! Take absolute sway! Give me the Holy Spirit!" (Day 136).

Suddenly, Moody felt that he was about to experience an infilling of the Spirit. Since he was near the home of a friend, he asked if he could find refuge from the spiritual storm that was gathering.

On his knees in a private room, Moody became a new man!

Moody was candid about this milestone. Dr. Day quoted a statement by him as recorded by Hartzler in *Moody in Chicago*: "I was in the church ten years before I knew anything especially about the Holy Spirit. When I heard a man . . . say that the Spirit was a person, I thought he was . . . daft. It is dreadful to see the powerless efforts of men trying to do spiritual work without spiritual power. . . . Men are turned against the gospel by workers without the energy and wisdom of the Holy Spirit. . . . *And The Holy Spirit coming upon men with power is distinct and separate from conversion.* I would rather go to breaking stones than to go into Christian work without the anointing of the Spirit" (128).

Having been baptized with the Spirit—many would call it sanctification—Moody's ministry expanded. Instead of winning hundreds, he began to win thousands. But one characteristic did not change. His grammar remained atrocious. He still said *ain't, tain't,* and *hain't!* Nonetheless, his have dids; have wents; and he don't knows, didn't hurt his ministry.

In 1882 Moody and Sankey held meetings at Cambridge

University. There, in spite of the fact that he persisted in referring to Daniel as Dannel, he made a solid impression; and it was through his influence that George Pilkington, C. T. Studd, and others were motivated to become missionaries.

This story of Moody illuminates several questions.

1. Did Moody have the Holy Spirit *before* his special infilling in Brooklyn? The answer is, Of course! The Book of Acts is explicit: "We are witnesses of these things; and so is also the Holy Ghost, whom God *hath given to them that obey him*" (5:32). And so is the Book of Romans. J. B. Phillips translated Romans 8:9 as follows: "You cannot, indeed, be a Christian at all unless you have something of the Holy Spirit within you."

Many biblical giants were greatly used by the Lord *after* a second touch. John Wesley had his Aldersgate experience *after* his conversion; George Pilkington had a second touch *after* he had read a book by a Tamil evangelist and waited on the Lord on the island of Kome. Charles Finney had a special infilling *after* he had surrendered to Christ—and Bishop James Hannington, like many others, testified to having his entire life transformed *after* reading a little book *Grace and Truth*, by Dr. Mackay.

The accounts of these experiences, we must admit, are rooted in personal incidents; and since, like the reformers, we must base our thinking on scripture alone, we ask, do we have biblical support for a second touch?

My answer, although questioned by many is, Of course!

One obvious scriptural answer comes from Mark 8:22-25. After Jesus had spit in the blind man's eyes, he asked him if he could see; and the man replied, "I see people; they look like trees walking around" (v. 24). But Jesus didn't want him to be only partially healed. "Once more Jesus put his hands on the man's eyes. Then his eyes were opened, his sight was restored, and he saw everything clearly" (v. 25). (These passages are from the NIV).

We also have the record of the twelve Ephesian disciples who had never even heard of the Holy Spirit (Acts 19:1-4). The fact that they were disciples indicates that they were believers. Even so, when asked, "Have you received the Holy Ghost since you believed?," they replied, "We have not so much as heard whether there be any Holy Ghost."

2. The next vital question, also a controversial one, is, Does one have to tarry in order to receive the baptism of the Holy Spirit? The answer is a definite no. The only record of anyone tarrying in the New Testament is on the Day of Pentecost.

After the twelve Ephesians expressed their ignorance of the Holy Spirit, Paul laid his hands on them, and immediately "the Holy Ghost came upon them; and they spake with tongues, and prophesied" (Acts 19:6).

Peter had a similar experience in the house of Cornelius as recorded in the tenth chapter of Acts. True, Cornelius was a godly man, was seeking truth, and had been fasting as he searched for truth (v. 30); but in no way could one say that he had been tarrying. Soon, as a result of the prayers of Cornelius, Peter visited his house, faced a large gathering, and preached.

"While Peter was still speaking . . . the Holy Spirit came on all who heard the message. The circumcised believers who had come with Peter were astonished that the gift of the Holy Spirit had been poured out even on the Gentiles, for they heard them speaking in tongues and praising God" (v. 44-46, NIV).

In that no one, other than for those who had the initial infilling on the Day of Pentecost, ever tarried and begged and pleaded for the Holy Spirit baptism, we wonder why thousands of people now tarry for hours in order to receive what they consider to be the second touch or the Holy Spirit's baptism?

Considering this problem, one who believes that all seekers should tarry, may refer to the experience of Dwight L. Moody. "Those dreadful women," it might be said, had prayed for Moody for a long time. Moreover, even after Moody was convinced, it was months before he had the experience.

3. Why did it take Moody so long before he had that

sacred experience that transformed his life? The answer is simple. While Moody was walking down the street on that cold November day, a wrestling match was going on in his heart. Strong willed, Moody had always insisted on doing things *his* way. Eventually as he walked along the sidewalk on that cold November day, the Lord won the battle and Moody held up the white flag of unconditional surrender. From the carefully guarded recesses of his being, he sobbed: "Oh God, why don't you *compel* me to walk close to thee, always? Deliver me from myself. Take absolute sway! Give me thy Holy Spirit."

It was at that moment of complete surrender that Moody had his revolutionizing experience with the Lord.

The lack of total surrender and our insistence on *the* gift that we desire are *the* major obstacles in our being baptized with the Spirit! Because of cheap grace, many, instead of relinquishing the treasure chests of their beings, have nothing more than a shallow, surface, usually noisy, religion.

After wiring his home, a frustrated member of the congregation approached me. "I turn on the switches, but nothing happens," he complained.

As I examined his wiring, I learned that he had followed the instructions of a book carefully. Puzzled, I went to the fuse box. It was in good shape. Then I made a startling discovery. *Instead of scraping the insulation from the heavily insulated wires when he connected them to the power, he had merely twisted the covered wires to the power,* and he had done the same thing at all the connections!

After I removed the insulation at each connection and twisted the *bare* wires together, and bared the wires before connecting them to each switch and outlet, he had plenty of light. Moreover, after this was done, we didn't beg the electricity to flow. It flowed instantly. Why? Because it's the nature of electricity to flow when all hindering conditions have been removed.

Let's notice two problems that keep believers from experiencing baptism or sanctification or the second blessing or whatever we want to call it.

1. Many have been convinced that the only evidence of having been baptized with the Holy Spirit is to speak in unknown tongues. Others insist that idea is not solid in scripture. They insist there are numerous occasions recorded in the New Testament where believers were baptized with the Spirit, and yet not a single word is mentioned about their speaking in unknown tongues. The outstanding example is Jesus Christ himself.

Does this mean that there is no such gift as speaking in tongues? Certainly not! Paul was emphatic: "Therefore, my brothers, be eager to prophesy, and do *not forbid* speaking in tongues" (1 Cor. 14:39, NIV).

Do modern believers in our dispensation ever speak in a tongue they do not understand? Certainly! While in Kenya my father was preaching through an interpreter. When the interpreter got sick I volunteered. But a few minutes later I got sick. Then an amazing thing happened. Not being a linguist, my father's Olinyore was hilarious.

By mixing several languages together, and mispronouncing the words in each language, he could make himself understood. But, in spite of that, he continued with his sermon in perfect Olinyore. It was miraculous.

Many have had similar and even more dramatic experiences. Paul's admonition at this point deserves profound consideration. "I would like everyone of you to speak in tongues, but I would rather have you prophecy. He who prophesies is *greater* than one who speaks in tongues, unless he interprets, so that the church may be edified" (1 Cor. 14:5, NIV).

J. B. Phillips rendered 1 Corinthians 14:5, "I should indeed like you to speak with 'tongues,' but I would much rather that you *all preached the Word of God.* For the preacher of the Word does a greater work than the speaker with 'tongues' unless of course the latter interprets his words for the benefit of the Church."

2. Believing that only the gift of tongues is evidence of having received the baptism of the Holy Spirit, many insist on going to great length to receive that gift.

This fact explains why so many who claim to have the gift of tongues do not. They've merely worked themselves into a frenzy. Counterfeits are a great hindrance to the work of the church and inspire many to insist that the gift of tongues is a sham.

Undoubtedly Paul was confronted with this problem at Corinth. As a result he devoted the entire twelfth chapter of 1 Corinthians to the subject of tongues.

When we study it, we observe that after he listed numerous gifts of the Spirit, he highlighted his argument with the eleventh verse: "All these are the work of one and the same Spirit, and he gives them to each one, *just* as he determines."

Since God has certain gifts for all those who meet his conditions, we should thankfully accept them, even though they may not include the gift of tongues! Paul concluded this chapter with a series of questions. "Do all have gifts of healing? Do all speak in tongues? Do all interpret? *But eagerly desire the greater gifts*" (vv. 30-31).

As we consider, and sometimes contend, over various points of view, we must acknowledge that probably no view is one hundred percent correct; and also that there are many who hold views contrary to ours who are being mightily used of the Lord.

Paul concluded the thirteenth chapter of First Corinthians: "Now we see but a poor reflection as in a mirror; then we shall see face to face. Now I know in part; then I shall know fully, even as I am fully known. Now these three remain: faith, hope and love. But the greatest of these is love" (vv. 12-13, NIV).

A danger in contending over doctrine is that we neglect the Holy Spirit. After all, he is anxious for the "streams of living water" promised by Jesus to flow from all believers. What's vitally important is not a specific view of his work; but rather that all of us, Pentecostal or non-Pentecostal, Charismatic or non-Charismatic, contenders for eradication and those who deny eradication be filled with his power. In the final analysis, the Holy Spirit will do precisely what the Spirit was assigned to do regardless of the shades of belief!

Can you answer?
1. What are three of the works of the Holy Spirit?
2. Why is Satan horrified by the power of the Holy Spirit?
3. Is speaking in tongues the only gift of the Holy Spirit?
4. Was Dwight L. Moody saved *before* his infilling?
5. Did Jesus speak in unknown tongues?
6. Do all spirit-filled Christians receive the same gifts?
7. Did Paul tarry before he was filled with the Holy Spirit?

Epilogue

Real spirituality is *doing* the will of Christ!
The greatest need of the church is not a better building, a higher steeple, a better trained choir, or better pews. Rather, it is a fresh baptism of the Holy Spirit. Paul believed in a constant renewal of the faith. His personal testimony was: "I die daily" (1 Cor. 15:31).

What can a Christian—any Christian—do in order to be baptized with the Holy Spirit? The first requirement for this blessing, call it what you will—the dedicated life, second-blessing holiness, sanctification, the baptism of the Holy Spirit—is to realize that it is for everyone. The *entire* group of "about 120" received this blessing on the Day of Pentecost. Moveover, "Jesus Christ is the same yesterday and today and forever" (Hebrews 13:8, NIV).

Having accepted this fact, we should then proceed to seek the experience. The best way I can explain the process of seeking *and* attaining the infilling is to use an object lesson.

During my teens while I was a missionary kid in Kenya, I built my own radio station with which I had two-way communication with seventy countries. The day I received my license after a long tussle with the Postmaster General, I turned the switch and sent out my first CQ. That call, which meant "anyone answer," was an exciting moment.

Having called CQ, I turned on my receiver and awaited an answer. In a moment, I heard a reply: "VQ4KSL this is VQ4SNB calling. Your signal is R7, QSA5 T4." In radio language that meant I was fairly loud, was quite readable, but the tone of my signal was very bad. In other words, instead of my signal being a perfect *dah dit dah dit*, it had a wobble in it and was being received in Songhor as *wobble dit wobble dit*. This was terrible and took away much of my joy of having had my first QSO (radio conversation).

VQ4SNB explained: Since your transmitter is a tuned-plate, tuned-grid affair, its wavelength can vary. And because your transmitter is on the table where your key is located, every time you press it, the table is jarred. Then the table jars the elements in your oscillator-tube; and that changes your wavelength and makes your signal go *wobble dit wobble dit*. You can cure this by putting your transmitter on a shelf.

I followed VQ4SNB's advice. That changed the tone of my signal from a T4 to a T7. Now, instead of going *wobble dit wobble dit*, it went *chirp dit chirp dit*. This was an improvement. Still I was not satisfied.

Then one day my signal dropped clear out of the Amateur Radio band. That was terrible. Afraid of losing my license, I explained my problem to VQ4SNB by mail!

His explanation was this: Even though your transmitter is on the shelf, the elements in the tube get hot, and that changes their characteristics. Because their characteristics are changed your wavelength changes. You need to change from self-control to crystal control.

After my studies confirmed his advice, I sent to England for a 7160 kilocycle crystal. That crystal was designed so that my transmitter could only work on one wavelength: 7160 kilocycles.

When the crystal arrived, I anxiously placed it between the brass plates on the transmitter. It didn't work. Additional study indicated that the crystal "sandwich" couldn't function unless the contacts were absolutely clean, and that they should only be cleaned with carbon tetrachloride.

The carbon tetrachloride did the trick. I was soon on the air again and my signal was reported to be T9X. The X meant that it was crystal controlled. From then on, instead of being self-controlled, my transmitter was crystal controlled. That tiny crystal, about the size of a quarter, was its new dictator and demanded that it work only on 7160 kilocycles.

How does this apply to having one's life taken over by the Holy Spirit?

1. When we are saved, our sins are forgiven. Nonetheless our wills have not generally been surrendered to the Holy

Spirit; and the Holy Spirit will not dominate and control our lives *unless* the Spirit is *allowed* to dominate and completely control them.

2. In order for the Holy Spirit to dwell within us, our lives must be clean; and the only way our lives can be clean is by repentance and faith in the cleansing power of the blood of Jesus Christ.

3. Having achieved the above, we must invite him to come in and exercise faith that the Lord's promises are true. After that we must *continue* to have faith that the Holy Spirit is dominating our lives in the same manner in which we continue to breathe oxygen. Also, we must continue to grow spiritually.

4. Those who are spirit-filled are frequently chastised by the Holy Spirit's counsel. Sometimes these chastisements are so sharp we cannot sleep. When this takes place, we should not allow Satan to insist that the Holy Spirit has left us. Rather, we should rejoice in knowing that the Holy Spirit is still with us and is merely doing his work in correcting and preparing us for the battles ahead.

Answers to Can You Answer?

Chapter 1
1. When God provided human beings with a soul.
2. To heal the sick and preach that "the kingdom of God is come nigh unto you" (Luke 10:9).
3. All members of the Trinity were present.
4. The Holy Spirit descended on Jesus in the form of a dove (Matt. 3:16). None of the witnesses to his baptism were named. A large crowd was probably present.
5. Jesus was "about thirty" (Luke 3:23) when he began his ministry.
6. The Acts of the Apostles merely records the highlights of the ministry of the apostles. The key word to Acts 1:1 is *began*. That word suggests the gospels and the Acts merely record the *beginning* of the works that were done by Jesus and the Twelve.
7. The sanitary conditions in Israel in the days of Jesus were terrible. Flies, human waste, and disease abounded. Many of the people like primitives in our time repeated incantations in order to drive away evil spirits and be healed.

Chapter 2
1. Julian tried to ruin Christianity with ridicule and by promoting division over doctrinal differences.
2. The letter was found in a boot of the murdered carrier—Linants de Bellefonds.
3. In Luganda *kabaka* means king. *Katikiro* means prime minister.
4. Pilkington was a brilliant linguist and pioneer missionary to Uganda.
5. Some Baganda learned to read upside down because they did not have enough copies of the New Testament.

Circled around a single copy, some viewed it upside down.
6. Pilkington was a deeply spiritual man and had consecrated his life many times before he was baptized with the Holy Spirit. His eyes were opened by reading a book on this subject by a Tamil evangelist.
7. Pilkington received the infilling of the Spirit while searching his heart on the island of Kome in Lake Victoria. The evidence that he had received the baptism was a new radiance, enthusiasm, and greatly increased success in his work.

Chapter 3
1. One reason that people don't swear by the Holy Spirit is that they are aware of Jesus' warning not to do so.
2. Kant was overwhelmed by (1) the starry heavens, (2) the moral law within.
3. Peter denounced Simon the Sorcerer, because he sought to enrich himself through the Good News of Jesus Christ.
4. The Holy Spirit is referred to by many names in the Bible (2 Cor. 3:18; Eph. 4:4; Heb. 9:14; 1 Pet. 4:14).
5. Scripture links the Holy Spirit with both God and Christ Acts 5:9; Acts 8:39; Acts 16:7; Romans 8:9; and 1 Peter 1:11.
6. The Holy Spirit is a person. The Spirit is never *it!*
7. Athanasius (296-374) was a small man with a keen mind. He tenaciously withstood Arius and his doctrine that Jesus was not coeternal with God.

Chapter 4
1. The first hint about the coming of Christ is in Genesis 3:15.
2. Victor Hugo considered the book of Job to be the greatest book ever written.
3. Job was inspired to write "my redeemer liveth" (19:25) by the Holy Spirit.
4. Job believed in immortality (Job 19:26).

5. A seraphim placed a live coal from off the altar on the lips of Isaiah (6:6).
6. Deborah gained the victory over Sisera by challenging Barak to attack him (Judges 4:4-14).
7. When the Twelve went out to preach, the only script they had with them was the Septuagint, the Greek translation of the Old Testament.

Chapter 5
1. The "schoolmaster" who points to Christ (Gal. 3:24) was the law of Moses.
2. At first, the Old Testament Feast of Pentecost was known as the Feast of Weeks (Exod. 34:22; Deut. 16:10).
3. Pentecost is so called because it was fifty days after Passover. The Greek word for fifty is *pentecostos*.
4. Before the exile, the first month of the Hebrew calendar (between March and April) was Abib—"month of the young ear." After the exile, Abib became Nisan—"beginning."
5. Jews eat bitter herbs at Passover to remind them of their bitter life during slavery. Bitter herbs include: lettuce, endive, barley; and, in modern times, horseradish. Unleavened bread is eaten to remind them of the hurry in which they escaped Egypt.
6. Since Pentecost is a joyous time, leaven is used.
7. A phylactery is a small leather box that contains the Hebrew texts: Exod. 13:1-10, 11-16 and Deut. 6:4-9; 11:13-21. It is secured by straps to the forehead and upper left arm.

Chapter 6
1. The "Last Supper" was on Thursday. Jesus was crucified on Friday.
2. Jesus washed the disciples feet *after* supper. John 13:2-4.
3. Jesus and the eleven disciples crossed the Kidron Valley.
4. The tombs were whitewashed so that no one would be accidentally defiled by touching one of them.

5. Only Peter, James, and John accompanied Jesus into Gethsemane.
6. Peter was in the courtyard of Caiaphas "about the space of one hour" (Luke 22:59).
7. Peter was accused of being a Galilean—"thy speech betrayeth thee" (Matt. 26:73).

Chapter 7
1. The Roman Governor was Pontius Pilate.
2. Jesus was tried by Herod Antipas, a son of Herod the Great.
3. Jesus did not open his mouth when he faced Herod. "he answered him nothing" (Luke 23:9).
4. Pilate tried three ways to escape making a decision concerning Jesus. (1) He sent him to Herod (Luke 23:7). (2) He had him chastised (Luke 23:16). (3) He asked the mob to decide whom he should release to them—Jesus Barabbas or Jesus Christ (Matt. 27:17).
5. John declared that Barabbas was a robber (18:40); Luke that he was wanted for sedition and murder (23:19); Mark that he had "committed murder in the insurrection" (15:7); and Matthew that he was a "notorious prisoner" (27:16).
6. Pilate had him "scourged" (Mark 15:15).
7. A Roman cross included the upright post—the *stipes*. The horizontal section was the *patibulum*.

Chapter 8
1. It was natural for Peter to doubt that Jesus did not have power to forgive sins because that is what he had been taught as a child. The scribes and Pharisees asked Jesus: "Who can forgive sins, but God alone?" (Luke 5:21).
2. Referring to the palsied man he had just healed, Jesus asked: "Which is easier: to say, 'Your sins are forgiven,' or to say 'Get up and walk'? " (Luke 5:23, NIV).
3. John the Baptist (John 1:29).
4. The Passover began on the Sabbath (Saturday) the 15th of Nisan.

5. John reached the tomb first (John 20:4).
6. The fire on which Jesus prepared the fish was of "burning coals" (21:9, NIV).
7. The hook refers to Jesus' call to Peter and Andrew: "Follow me, and I will make you fishers of men" (Matt. 4:19). The crook reminds us that Peter was to "feed my sheep" (John 21:17). Sheep herders carried a staff with a crook on the end.

Chapter 9
1. Jesus commanded them: "Do not leave Jerusalem, but wait for the gift my Father promised, which you have heard me speak about. For John baptized with water, but in a few days you will be baptized with the Holy Spirit" (Acts 1:4-5, NIV).
2. While in the flesh, Jesus remained on earth forty days.
3. On the Mount of Olives (Acts 1:9-12).
4. Those who gathered in Jerusalem to wait for the promise were about 120 (Acts 1:15).
5. G. Campbell Morgan came to the conclusion that the 120 lingered in the temple by comparing Luke 24:52, 53; Acts 1:14; Acts 2:1; Acts 2:46.
6. The two candidates who sought to fill the place of Judas among the twelve were "Barsabbas, who was surnamed Justus, and Matthias" (Acts 1:23).
7. The Feast of Pentecost was celebrated in the spring.

Chapter 10
1. Since Jesus died a few hours before the Passover; appeared to his disciples over a period of "forty days" (Acts 1:3); and since Pentecost is fifty days after Passover, the 120 had waited approximately ten days.
2. The only scriptures the 120 had available for study were either the Hebrew Old Testament or its Greek translation—the Septuagint.
3. The sound from heaven like "a rushing mighty wind" (Acts 2:2) appealed to their sense of hearing; "the cloven tongues like as of fire" (v. 3) appealed to their sense of

sight; the chairs on which they sat, appealed to their sense of touch; the smell of incense and smoke from the altar appealed to their sense of smell, and the savor of the food appealed to their sense of taste.
4. The bread at Pentecost was made of wheat.
5. The tongues of fire at Pentecost reminded those who watched of the "burning bush" witnessed by Moses (Exod. 3:2).
6. The Greek word for tongues is *glossolalia*.
7. On the Day of Pentecost "there were added unto them about three thousand souls" (Acts 2:41).

Chapter 11
1. After the doors were closed to Paul and his friends in Bithynia, they went to Philippi in Macedonia.
2. Phillips Brooks authored "O Little Town of Bethlehem."
3. On the Day of Pentecost the sense of hearing was appealed to three times: (1) by the sound like a mighty rushing wind; (2) those who spoke in the many languages used; (3) Peter's sermon.
4. Mary, mother of Jesus, was among the 120.
5. Madam Schuman-Heink was stopped from committing suicide by her daughter.
6. The Mayflower Compact was adopted by the pilgrims because instead of landing in Virginia where they would have been under the laws of England, they had landed at what is now Provincetown, Massachusetts, where there were no European laws.
7. Peter and Paul were opposites in many ways. Peter was a fisherman, Paul was a tentmaker. Paul was highly educated; Peter was not. Peter had known Jesus in the flesh; Paul had not.

Chapter 12
1. The Holy Spirit has many duties: (1) he convicts humanity of sin. "When he comes, he will convict the world of guilt in regard to sin and righteousness and judgment" (John 16:9, NIV); (2) he intercedes: "But the

Spirit himself intercedes for us with groans that words cannot express" (Romans 8:26, NIV); (3) he gives power: "Not by might, nor by power, but by my spirit saith the Lord of hosts" (Zech. 4:6).
2. Satan fears the Holy Spirit because he is not equal to the Holy Spirit.
3. Speaking in tongues is only one gift of the Spirit.
4. Moody was saved even before he had heard of the Holy Spirit.
5. There is no record that Jesus ever spoke in an unknown tongue.
6. All Spirit-filled Christians do not receive the same gifts. "There are different kinds of gifts, but the same Spirit" (1 Cor. 12:4).
7. Paul did not tarry before he was filled with the Spirit. Acts 9:17-18 states that after Ananias prayed that he receive his sight "and be filled with the Holy Ghost . . . *immediately* there fell from his eyes as it had been scales: and he received his sight forth with, and arose and was baptized."

Notes

Chapter 2
1 Uganda means the country. Luganda, the language. Buganda, the kingdom; Baganda, the people, and Muganda a person.

Chapter 3
1 To this exclamation, Phillips added this explanation: "These words are exactly what the Greek means. It is a pity that their real meaning is obscured by modern slang usage."
2 A *Discourse Concerning the Holy Spirit* by John Owen. Philadelphia: Protestant Episcopal Book Society, 1862, p. 56. Quoted by John Walvoord, in *The Holy Spirit*, p. 37.

Chapter 8
1 The KJV adds: "and of an honeycomb."
2 Undoubtedly the word *eleven* referred to the group, *not* the number.

Bibliography

Albright, Raymond W. *Focus on Infinity*. Macmillan, 1961.
Ashe, R. P. *Chronicles of Uganda*. Hodder and Stoughton, 1894.
Battersby, C. F. *Pilkington of Uganda*. Marshall Brothers Pubs. n.d.
Beldon, Albert D. *George Whitefield—The Awakener*. Cokesbury Press, 1930.
Berry, W. G. *Bishop Hannington, A Missionary Hero*.
Bloch, Abraham P. *The Biblical and Historical Background of Jewish Holy Days*. Ktav Publishing House, Inc. 1978.
Bowersock, G. W. *Julian the Apostate*. Cambridge: Harvard U. Pr., 1978.
Brand, Paul and Phillip Yancy. *Fearfully and Wonderfully Made*. Grand Rapids, Mich: Zondervan, 1980.
Bruce, F. F. *The Gospel of John*. Grand Rapids, Mich: Eerdmans, 1983.
Carnegie, Dale. *Five Minute Biographies*. Blue Ribbon Books, 1937.
Churchill, Winston S. *Their Finest Hour*. Boston: Houghton, Mifflin, 1949.
Cummings, J. E. *Through the Eternal Spirit*. S. W. Partridge and Co. n.d.
Day, Albert. *Bush Aglow*. Valley Forge, Penn: Judson Press, 1936.
Edersheim, Alfred. *Life and Times of Jesus the Messiah*. Hendrickson (n.d.).
Edersheim, Alfred. *The Temple: Its Ministry and Services*. Grand Rapids, Mich: Eerdmans, 1950.
Greenstone, Julius H. *Jewish Feasts and Fasts*. Palm Springs, Calif: Block Pub. Co., 1946.
Hunter, J. A. & Daniel Mannix. *Tales of the African Frontier*. New York: Harper, 1954.
Ludwig, Charles. *At the Cross*, Warner, 1989.

—*At the Tomb*, Warner, 1991.
—*Ludwig's Handbook of New Testament Rulers and Cities*. Accent, 1983.
—*Queen of the Reformation*. Minneapolis: Bethany, 1986.
Morgan, G. Campbell. *The Acts of the Apostles*, Old Tappan, NJ: Revell, 1924.
Muggeridge, Malcolm. *Confessions of a Twentieth Century Pilgrim*. Harper, 1988.
Owen, John. *A Discourse Concerning the Holy Spirit*. Philadelphia: Protestant Episcopal Book Society, 1862.
Porter, David. *The Practical Christianity of Malcolm Muggeridge*. Downer's Grove, Ill: Inter-Varsity, 1984.
Seaver George. *David Livingstone, His Life and Letters*. Harper, 1957.
Schlossberg, Herbert. *Called to Suffer Called to Triumph*. Multnomah, 1990.
Thomas, Henry and Dana Lee. *Living Biographies of Great Composers*. Garden City Publishing Co., 1940.
Walvoord, John F. *The Holy Spirit*. Van Kampen Press, 1954.
Wesley, John. *The Works of John Wesley*. Zondervan. n.d.